THE
TRUTH
BOOK

THE
TRUTH
BOOK

*Escaping a Childhood of Abuse
among Jehovah's Witnesses*

A Memoir

JOY CASTRO

ARCADE PUBLISHING
NEW YORK

For my brother

FIRST EDITION

To preserve privacy, several names have been changed or omitted.

Library of Congress Cataloging-in-Publication Data

Castro, Joy.
    The truth book : escaping a childhood of abuse among Jehovah's Witnesses :
a memoir / by Joy Castro. —1st ed.
    p. cm.
ISBN 1-55970-787-9
1. Castro, Joy—Family. 2. Castro, Joy—Childhood and youth. 3. English teachers—United States—Biography. 4. Children of divorced parents—United States—Biography. 5. Abused children—United States—Biography. 6. Jehovah's Witnesses—Biography. 7. Stepfathers—United States. I. Title.

PE64.C37A3 2005
420'.92—dc22   2005010304

Published in the United States by Arcade Publishing, Inc., New York
Distributed by Time Warner Book Group

Visit our Web site at www.arcadepub.com

10 9 8 7 6 5 4 3 2 1

Designed by API

EB

PRINTED IN THE UNITED STATES OF AMERICA

She was saved in that she was hopeful.

—Theodore Dreiser, *Sister Carrie*

and, in the end,
this isn't a poem about foolishness
but about how I rose from the ground
and saw the world as if for the second time
the way it really is.

—Mary Oliver, from "Alligator Poem"

ACKNOWLEDGMENTS

The prologue first appeared under the title "What She Told Me When I Found Her" in *Hip Mama* #33, the Outcast Issue (2005).

A portion of chapter 5 first appeared as "Clips of My Father's House" in *Wabash Magazine* (Winter/Spring 2001) and in *Key West: A Collection* (2001).

Portions of chapters 6, 7, 8, 10, and 11 first appeared under the title "Farm Use" in *Without a Net: The Female Experience of Growing Up Working Class* (2003).

Lines from "Alligator Poem" from *New and Selected Poems* by Mary Oliver. Copyright © 1992 by Mary Oliver. Reprinted by permission of Beacon Press, Boston.

Line from "The soul selects her own society" reprinted by permission of the publishers and the Trustees of Amherst College from *The Poems of Emily Dickinson*, Thomas H. Johnson, ed., Cambridge, Mass.: The Belknap Press of Harvard University Press, Copyright © 1951, 1955, 1979, 1983 by the President and Fellows of Harvard College.

"I Want To Be Somebody's Baby" by Barry Manilow and Enoch Anderson © Careers-BMG Music Publishing, Inc. (BMI) and

Catapult Music (BMI). All rights for the world on behalf of Catapult Music (BMI) administered by Careers-BMG Music Publishing, Inc. (BMI).

Lines from "Mending Wall" from *The Poetry of Robert Frost*, edited by Edward Connery Lathem. Published by Henry Holt and Company, 1969, New York.

THE
TRUTH
BOOK

PROLOGUE:

What My Mother Told Me When I Found Her

I was alone in Miami then, staying with a girlfriend who'd gotten married. Her husband didn't want me there, didn't know me, claimed I was a bad influence on the children. At night, they'd argue.

"It won't be much longer," my friend would say. "October."

The abortion hadn't worked. Lenny had driven me to the industrial park in Peoria. I gave the man our two hundred dollars. He didn't look like a doctor. He took me to a room farther back in the warehouse while Lenny waited on a folding chair. He told me to close my eyes and relax. He put things in me and took them out, played around down there. Then he told me to go home. It hadn't seemed so bad. Lenny drove to Chinatown and we ate dinner. I sat with my head on his shoulder all the way home. He'd let me, now. He was affectionate again, now that I'd done it.

But nothing happened. It was still in there, and we had no more money. My mother, the only other person in Rockford who knew, said my father would beat me to death if he found out. He'd beaten me before. I'd seen him beat my brothers. I left the farm alone.

I took buses to Miami and took a job in a hospital, planning nutritious meals for Seventh-Day Adventists. I bought a ring to wear so people wouldn't ask questions. This was 1967, you understand.

1

Sometimes even married women had to leave their jobs when they started to show.

My friend wanted to adopt the baby, but she slapped her kids. I didn't want that. She drank, too. I'd wake up early with the children and give them breakfast while she slept it off.

I wandered the hot streets. Sometimes I'd sit in playgrounds and watch the mothers with their children. I folded my left hand over my right so my ring would show and I could sit there without embarrassment. The women were nice. It was like a club. They'd chat with me on the benches, and I'd say how far along I was and lie about my husband and our little bungalow in Hialeah and how we hoped you'd love the beach as much as we did.

I used to wait for the city bus at a shopping center, what we call strip malls now. Sometimes I'd walk through the stores for the shade and large cooling fans, the soothing whir they made. Once, I stopped in a long aisle like a tunnel, and rising on both sides around me, extending on metal arms from the pegboard, were baby clothes: yellow chenille cardigans, no bigger than my outstretched hand, with happy ducks sewn on; the warm fuzz of receiving blankets, pink and blue; tiny white dresses with eyelet ruffles; soft small socks like pockets for a thumb, their cuffs rimmed in lace. I knew you'd be a girl. Against the thin skin of my belly I could feel you moving as I ran my hands across those fine little things. Delicate, they were so delicate, the crocheted booties, the little colored tights, so small and soft and bright in the dim high tunnel of the aisle, so light and flimsy. I stood there, stroking for what seemed like the longest time, feeling their softness collapsing against my fingers and your strange push inside me. I couldn't leave, couldn't move, couldn't imagine the man and woman who would buy these things for you.

"Ma'am," the clerk said, suddenly beside me, clearing his throat, "do you need some help?"

1

From the street, the houses of Marrakech are anonymous. Flat, blank walls intermittently broken by doors, they reveal nothing, have all the allure of a massive shipping center, windowless, set back from the highway near a small town where the residents celebrate the influx of jobs and try to think no further.

But entering a house in Marrakech, you find doors inlaid with shell and brass, carved and painted ceilings jutting down in three dimensions, their sculpted surfaces lacquered red and ocher. Turquoise. Black. A fireplace tiled in intricate designs, walls of *tadelakt*, hidden courtyards with palms rising higher than the roof, low burning lamps beside still pools. Through the arched door is the bedroom, the bed with its thick cool damask. Close your eyes. A fountain bubbles, splashes. The darkness of the room is green.

When you awake, you see unfurled across the carved bedframe the thousand painted names of God.

In San Cristóbal de las Casas, in Chiapas, the walls of houses on the street are nearly featureless. Old Spanish fortifications against the Mayans, they stand a foot thick. Between them, the steep stone-paved roads are narrow, the width of one U.S. lane and its shoulder.

The sidewalks, built from the same white or tan or pale gold stone, rise a foot above the street and are wide enough for only one person. You edge around strangers, your bodies brushing.

The light is fierce, astonishing. Everyone squints. The walls are painted white, mustard, red, sea blue. Only vertical paint lines, wavering, mark the approximate end of one house, the beginning of another. Now red glows against your face as you walk, now white again, now peach. Here a shard of stucco has broken away, and you can see the thick mud packed inside. You walk single file through a maze of walls of glazed mud, claustrophobes with only the stone and sky to stare at.

In the zócalo, the town square, everything is open, free, for sale. There's the park, the gazebo, the outdoor café with its lacy iron benches. Trees grow in plain sight. There are the stores and government buildings, their doors open, their walls full of windows, the shutters pinned back. Buy stamps. Buy film. This is where people go to see and be seen, where couples promenade at dusk, where children cluster to sell you woven bracelets.

But what you want — you feel it like an urge, a need — is to go back, between those thick, concealing walls, their tall wooden doors blackened on the other side by centuries of soot, their heavy iron hardware clanking as they shut behind you.

Inside, low ceilings slant, burnt orange, over divans thick with embroidery. The white hearth curves smooth as an egg from its white wall. You sink to the tiled floors of courtyards rioting with bougainvillea — hot pink, purple, mango — and fountains, pools, the spiked or tumbling green plants like oases in a hot, bright clime. Lush, wet, cool, hushed. The lovemaking spins out across an afternoon. Soft blurred voices echo from a room you cannot see.

It is a different kind of architecture. A world of privacy.

It is 1997. I am twenty-nine and on the market. In a few months, I'll have my doctorate. My dissertation isn't finished. It's too early, my advisors say, to interview: Wait a year; have your degree in hand, an offer for your revision from a good university press. But my advisors don't remember being desperate. Another year is another year at $12,000, another year of mounting debt, a son who'll be that much older, that much trickier to transplant.

I have five interviews in D.C. This is good; there are between four and eight hundred applicants for each of the forty-five positions for which I apply, carefully tailoring my letter and vita each time. In my department, only one graduate student has more interviews: a composition specialist who's taught in the prison system and has an edgy dissertation about the correlations between the institution of the prison and the institution of the university. After me, the next literature person has one interview, and gets no offer. It's a dismal business.

My interviews, though, go well, all held in rooms in various D.C. hotels more posh than I can afford, where the interviewers and I pretend not to notice that we're perched on the edges of double beds. One interview is lovely, three are all right, and one is dreadful, with the aging department chair visibly dozing, the untenured Young Turk firing sarcastic questions. I'd read his book (on sado-masochism), and it was smart; he deserved to be sarcastic, I supposed. And I'd found the chair's novel dull, too, so everything seemed to fit.

Three schools invite me for the coveted final flyback.

The campus interviews take place in February. My black loafers, used to Texas, see snow. I break the bank to buy a second outfit, a gray wool jacket and a plaid wool skirt on sale. The skirt has no lining. Throughout, I itch in places I cannot scratch.

Each night when I'm dropped off at my motel, or bed-and-breakfast with a view of the bay, or exquisite historical home on campus, I strip and flop on the bed, eating a PowerBar, ravenous because I've been answering questions all through the interviews, breakfast, lunch, and dinner. In between, there have been the polished presentation of research, the guest-teaching of a professor's course-in-progress, and the meetings with the dean, the president, the department chair, and each member of the department, who all ask such similar questions that everything starts to blur.

At the first campus, a West Coast university, a student yells, "I'm a radical lesbian feminist Jew, and what are you going to do about that?"

I say I'll read her work and give her honest critical feedback — a reply that doesn't satisfy her. A member of the faculty, her interest piqued by my surname, wants to know if I'm the child of migrant farmworkers and loses interest when I'm not.

The final flyback will be the place of the lovely interview: polite, interesting, engaged, professional. But I'm reluctant to go because it's a men's college, one of only three left in the country. It's a small liberal arts school with a good academic reputation, which I want, but it's conservative, and I don't know what that combination might mean for my scholarship on leftist women writers. It turns out to be the job I take.

But the invitation to the middle interview comes as a surprise. It's the dreadful one, the dozing chair and Young Turk at a college with a national reputation and a good research library. I'm eager to do well.

Everything has gone smoothly. It's almost over. I've made it through my research presentation, through teaching Robert Browning and Matthew Arnold — not my field — and through the surreal first dinner at the chair's own house, where I was seated at a table in the kitchen and handed a strange tool.

"Ever pit olives?" the chair said, and thunked a large bowl of black ones in front of me.

The arrival of guests had not helped. The young fiction writer and her boyfriend, both of whom I liked, talked quietly only to each other; the poet talked about her sex life and divulged — had we any idea? — the size of whale penises. The Victorianist and her husband seemed tense. Much wine was passed around, and voices became loud. No one asked about my work, my teaching. I tried to ask about theirs, but I'd been seated between two faculty wives who stayed home with their children, so we talked about that.

The night grew long. Corks lay stained between the plates and dishes. Finally, the chair's wife, laughing loudly, placed her forehead on the table and slapped the wood several times. Her forehead remained there, and she continued to laugh. This seemed to indicate the end of dinner.

I was driven back to my run-down hotel, where truckers propositioned me in the lobby and the elevator shuddered on its way up. It seemed all of a piece.

So I am relieved to learn that the final dinner will take place in public, at a restaurant, and that the chair and his wife will not attend. The Young Turk is telling me this, pulling into the hotel parking lot. I'll have an hour of solitude first in which to scratch my thighs.

"A word of advice," he says as I gather my things from the floor of his car. "If you *do* have a personality, tonight's dinner would be a good time to let it show."

I stare.

"I beg your pardon?"

"Your teaching's fine. Your research is fine, interesting — well, not great, but okay. The students like you. But we're all wondering if you have, you know, a *personality*." He snickers.

I don't notice that I am crossing the parking lot or pressing the elevator button. My thoughts pound. Perhaps he is right. I *am* reserved, shy. *Although quiet in seminar discussion,* begin sentences in my recommendation letters. Serious. I like to listen and think.

Perhaps they're right. I'd always just assumed I had a personality, and perhaps I didn't — as in the journals of the novelist Jean Rhys, when she enjoys a second wind of success in old age, and a fan of her early work confronts her, sure she is dead. Rhys wrote, *You think, "Perhaps I am."*

I had wanted to be an attentive lens, transparent. Perhaps I'd overdone it, becoming invisible altogether. Become colorless, when I'd meant to be clear.

I sit on the edge of the bed for some time, staring at the drawn drapes. The hour is slipping away. I call Cara, my best friend back home. I am newly married and would like to call my husband, but if I do have no personality, I'd rather he didn't find out just yet.

As soon as I start to speak, I am gulping, crying with shame. I tell her what the Young Turk said. It all seems so terrible and true. She does what a friend does, says, "Fuck him," several times, reminds me of when I've made her laugh, generous things I've done. I'm doubtful. But I press a cold washcloth to my eyes and brush my hair.

The poet, the senior fiction writer, and I dine in a green-and-white restaurant, fake ivy stapled onto lattice. I try explaining the pedagogical approaches that have already won two university teaching awards. The poet talks of her sex life and her breakups.

Finally, the two writers are talking only to each other, and the good white wine in their glasses ebbs and rises with the waiter's every pass. The poet puts her head on the senior writer's shoulder, whispers, confides, cries a little. I push the strands of pasta around my plate.

I get no offer from that school, though interviewing is so awful in a hilarious, bleak way, I would have accepted one. None of their candidates gets an offer that season.

The following year, they hire a brilliant woman in my field. I've read her book and admired it. It is a better scholarly book than I will ever write: dense with information, rich with nuanced readings, leavened by her graceful, intelligent prose. I cannot find a flaw. All this, and personality, too, I presume. Good luck to you, my dear. May your olives have no pits.

At the school where I am hired, the men's college, I replace a legend, a man who once drove his motorcycle through the administration building, who was given to using *fuck* in the classroom and freely dispensing F's in order to make students strive harder. Once, campus security rang his home in the middle of the night to report that his office had been ransacked. He arrived, sleepy: "No, no. This is how I left it." Chaotic, unbound. He moved for a while to a primitive cabin without facilities, appalling colleagues with his aroma. At faculty meetings, no one wanted to sit next to him. He'd moved with his wife and small daughter to live in China for a time, to avoid complacency.

His corner office, which I inherit, has two windows, beautiful hardwood floors, and acid orange walls — to keep people from feeling too settled, he says. I ask maintenance to please paint them cream. Smooth, obliterating layers roll over his legacy — like tanks over a free country, a Young Turk might say.

Academia now is different from the old, good life of sherry in the afternoons and leather-patched elbows. I know the competition. I work long hours, treat the students kindly, read my papers at conferences, and do not say *fuck* in class. I order books by the women writers of my period, which the library has never been asked to purchase, tally the numbers on my course evaluations, prepare neat dossiers for my reviews, sit through long meetings where I'm the only person in a skirt or under fifty.

Without orange paint or China, I've never felt complacent. Only the lucky ones roar through on their engines, cause a ruckus, throw champagne flutes over their shoulders. And they don't realize they're lucky, with great nets of family, love, hubris, or money to catch them. They think, instead, that we're dull. Despite his dazzling way with a sentence, I've never been moved by Fitzgerald, whom my predecessor taught each spring. The characters he cares about do yearn — oh, they yearn — but they yearn selfishly, shallowly. They never give anything, never succeed in saving anyone. They're the people I cleaned up after when I worked in a hotel. Callous, wealthy, all infatuated with one another's glamour, they glimmer like pearls draped down Nicole Diver's golden back, like Daisy's laugh full of money. Who's watching their children?

It's the show of it all that gets to me, I suppose, the display, the gaudy nights, the wineglass filling and refilling, the drunk hand smacking the table, the glittering public parade of one's thoughts and evanescent moods, like a suburban house decked out for Christmas, its thousand lights on plastic grids draped over the shrubs, blinking, flashing, the poor faded plastic reindeer glowing from within, their innards lit for anyone passing on the street.

Sometimes there may be reasons that a person is reserved. She may be dreaming, for example, of Marrakech, of the *riyad,* or of intricate prayer towers made by hand, each drawer latched with a silk thong and a sliver of bone, opening to reveal a tiny scroll.

We roll things up to protect them. The words rustle against the inner curls of parchment. When forcibly unrolled, they recoil. *The Soul selects her own Society*—, wrote Emily Dickinson, *Then — shuts the Door*—. Used to lying dormant, unread, secure, such scrolls whisper to themselves in the dark, murmuring of sunlit stone streets, tall blackened doors opening only by invitation into solace, intricacy, luxury, the lilt of the fountain, the wet, lush, cool green pool couched in the garden, safe within thick anonymous walls, with only a shift in the tint of paint to demarcate me from you.

2

The night before my father shoots himself, I have a dream.

My son and I hunker in the basement, listening to the siren and the storm. We have quilts, jugs of water, everything we can gather to keep ourselves safe. I look out the window. It's coming. It doesn't have the slender curvature of my usual tornado — silver, sure, deranged, hunting me through crowded streets, the spun roulette wheel whose game is the game of chance, the held breath. No. This tornado is a wall, a mass, a gray wave wide as a town. There will be no evasion, no artful dodge. This one will hit.

We've done all we can to prepare. I raise my empty hand as if raising a glass to toast, giddy, delirious with fear. "If we make it through this one, we're going to make it," I say to Grey, who is thirteen in this dream, his real age — not a toddler, not an infant, not my brother — and he raises his invisible glass back at me. Smiling. Sanguine.

It is the last of a week's run of tornado dreams, the first such dreams I've had since I was twenty-six, since the adoption registry called with the name of a woman they thought could be my mother. (All that month I hunch over my son in the night as tornadoes sweep through. One hovers over me, its silvery mouth yawning as I look up and fall upside down into its arms, my son shrinking on the ground

11

above me. At the Milwaukee airport, an orange-haired woman in owl glasses picks me up, rushing me at the gate as I stagger in her arms. But she cannot be mine; we look nothing alike: a horrible mistake has been made. I accede to everything, wondering how to escape. Driving me to her house, she talks about something, but her hands on the steering wheel leap suddenly into my vision, swallow the freeway, the buildings, the world: they are my hands. Older. But my hands, for the first time in my life. I stare in wonder at her frizzed hair. At the house, her son and daughter greet me, and I see my dark eyebrows spanning their faces like wings, their dark hair, their huge dark eyes she knew me by. That night, while I'm asleep and dreaming in their guest bed, a tornado lifts me like a sister, gentle as a breath, steady, like a cable car over the mountains, and deposits me on a strange rooftop where the weather's fine.)

Now, for the first time in eight years, something's coming. I think through the map of possible threats, disasters. My brother's well; no problems there. My mother, the one who raised me, has lain dormant for years in her third marriage, not responding to my calls. I search for my stepfather's name on the Internet, search archives of West Virginia newspapers to read again of his arrest, trial, imprisonment, to find when he was released, to see if he's been sent back for some new crime, but there's no news. I search obituaries, hopeful that he's died, and find nothing but the death notice of Mrs. Boggess, eighty-eight, my middle school home economics teacher. The dreams keep coming.

They end with my stepmother's voice on the phone: *I'm sorry to have to tell you this* — my knees buckling just at her tone, so scared and solemn — *but your father took his life this afternoon* — and then I am doubled, wails pouring, howls rushing out, and it occurs to me to wonder why our neighbors do not come to check — it's a hot July day, the windows are open, Grey has closed himself in his room, he doesn't know why I'm sobbing, what's wrong — that the tornado has hit.

I'm not the only one: Aunt Lettie, my father's older sister, the one who took him with her to the Key West five-and-dime — she dreams. As a child, he'd sit on the stool for hours, ordering one sandwich, then another, chewing his sister's handiwork as she stood behind the counter in her crisp uniform and coral lipstick. My father loved to see us eat when we were little. In his abandoned house after the funeral, we find an album of snapshots from one of his visits to my home in Texas. Grey's five. My father takes him miniature golfing, to his ballet class, out for frozen yogurt. He takes four shots of Grey in love with a white plastic spoon, eyes half closed with sugar rapture.

Aunt Lettie dreams of him all that week before, strange night-dreams that heave her up into consciousness, leave her staring out the kitchen window with a cup cooling in her hand, wondering if Lee won't just show up someday, pull up in his RV and say he's spending the weekend. She thinks in wonder, *I haven't thought of him in months.* She tells me this on the phone a couple of days after he dies, her sharp staccato tones like Nanny's, rapid-fire in English like Nanny's were in Spanish. She talks: about her old job at the bank, her old job with a dentist, her old job at a Publix Supermarket, about how she hasn't left the house at night since 1993 ("I don't even know what this town *looks* like at night!"), how she and my mother once were friends, how they would stay up all night, talking and drinking and talking.

Crumpled on the splintery bare wood floor of our upstairs office, I can see them, with their dark curls and long slim dancers' legs crossed at the knee under the kitchen table, their Kinos dangling from their toes. Insouciant. Their cigarettes waving gracefully in their long elegant women's fingers, before my mother quit. "I never had a friend like your mother," Lettie's voice raps out, tangy in my ear like the voice of no one in the Midwest where I live. "No one understood me like she did."

After the divorce, Lettie called her. My mother broke down, she was so grateful. She'd thought Lettie would hate her. "And I said to your mother, 'But I'm not a Jehovah's Witness anymore. I've been disfellowshipped, too, you know. For smoking cigarettes, same as Lee.' Your mother's voice changed entirely, got hard, you know, professional. 'Well, then I can't talk to you,' she said, and hung up. She hung up on me!" Twenty-two years ago. The sting's still in her voice.

"I'm sorry," I say. I am. My mother won't write, won't speak to me, either. For a while, it was intermittent, depending on how fawning I was, or how worldly my behavior seemed. Now, nothing for years.

I wonder if Lettie will mention my father again, or if the quick remarks at the beginning —"I'm so sorry, dear. We all are"— are all she can bear.

I think what I'd do if my little brother killed himself, what words I would be unable to say. I sit on the rough, soft wood floor, curling the telephone cord in and out between my toes while my aunt, the one who remembers him best as a child, speaks quickly of unrelated things.

Not like Aunt Lou, who can't stop sobbing to speak, calling from Key West. "I just know how much you adored your father," she says. "And how he adored you." It's true. *But not enough,* I think.

My brother Tony flies up with his girlfriend, Cool Julie, from Austin, where he's a mechanic. We'll drive over together in a van: the two of them, me, my husband, Grey. They put their bags on the sleeping porch. That night I'm crying in the backyard, hard, desperate, silent, clutching my own arms. Tony comes out for a smoke.

"Hey, you," he says.

I'm furious, helpless. "I want to protect you. And I can't."

He grabs and holds my arms, looks in my eyes. "No, you can't protect me from this one. You don't have to." He's laughing, but his eyes are wet. "I love it that you still want to protect me, but you can't." He's twenty-nine. His arms are bigger around than mine, I notice. He's maybe a little taller. "Not this time. We've got to help each other through this one," he says.

We stand in the darkness, then, talking quietly: what it means, the funeral, what our father's wishes were, what we need to do. The kitchen is four rectangles of light behind him. We're enclosed by the perfume of soft pink cabbage roses around our knees, the sprawling wands of the butterfly bushes, hovering near our shoulders, the scent of their dense violet plumes. There's a soft night wind that stirs things. It's pretty weird, we agree in the darkness. A pretty ironic thing: our father was the good parent, the one we could count on.

3

We were forced to stand naked in front of the guard. The sentence shocks and sticks, crystalline, in my five-year-old brain. It's in the *Yearbook of Jehovah's Witnesses,* which I impress my mother by reading on my own. It's a report on the persecution and concentration camps in Malawi. Malawi is where our prayers go each Sunday morning, Tuesday evening, and Thursday night, there in Africa with our brothers and sisters, persecuted for Jehovah's name's sake. From the upstairs of a converted carriage house in Surrey, England, which serves as our Kingdom Hall, our thoughts fly to comfort our brothers and sisters in distress.

The upstairs is warm and comfortable and droning. The downstairs, where the bathroom is, is frigid, painted a fluorescent peach. The walls are damp and cold as I touch them going down.

We were forced to stand naked in front of the guard. At home, I pore over the sentence. Something in it has clicked for me, something bad, something erotic, something about helplessness. Women were forced to stand naked in front of male guards who, after inspecting them, it says, slashed their buttocks with a whip. We're always told we could be punished like that at any time, persecuted for Jehovah, and that we should be glad to suffer for his name's sake.

There is something terrible and fearful and exciting about it all, like the scene on British television where men in olden-days clothes hold down a struggling woman and force a long red tube between her lips, down her throat. My father walks into the room and switches it off, leaves. I struggle to think what it could mean. I play Concentration Camp in the bathtub, pretending it's a train car. We've learned about Nazis, how Jehovah's Witnesses were killed in the camps with the Jews. How we need to be ready to go at any time.

My mother is pleased I am reading the yearbook by myself, that I am drawn to it. It bodes well for my spiritual growth.

At night I suck my finger frantically, rub my silky white blanket over my nose and lips. I am like one of those test monkeys placed in a cage with a mother made only of terrycloth and wire. I suck my finger, sniff the dried saliva. It's the smell of warmth, musk, intimacy, the smell I recognize years later on lovers' skin after sex. The smell of the breast, perhaps, to a sated baby.

My mother scolds me for being sensitive. *Melodramatic* is one of her words. When I say the bathwater is too hot, sometimes she will add cold water and swish her hand back and forth in the tub, but sometimes she pushes me down into it, holding me there by my arms. When I say the hairbrush hurts, she clamps me between her knees and keeps brushing. "Sing a song," she says. "Sing a song about how much it hurts." The hairbrush yanks my head back. "Just quit your whining." I cannot stand the wool sweater against my skin and cry to have it taken off. She says I'd better learn to like it. *Hypersensitive,* another of her words.

I am a difficult child to raise, she says. Annoying. Always underfoot. And *slow as molasses in January.*

Terror is the feeling: I am three, and the Kingdom Hall's dun-colored walls and steam heat bear down when she walks up the aisle, away from me, onto the stage, and sits and talks into the microphone on

17

its long silver stalk. She talks to the other seated woman. They bend their heads over black Bibles open in their laps and say things in friendly voices, reading scriptures to each other and nodding.

All alone I sit in the middle of the empty row, alone for the first time, my mother so far away. Her body is like my body, I cannot be away from it, I don't know what will happen or how long it will last. I start whimpering, I cannot help it. The Hancock girls twist around to stare, three blond heads swiveling, their mother tapping Sylvia on the leg to make her sit up straight and pay attention. A woman I don't know moves over next to me in the row behind and touches my shoulder. She hands me a butterscotch. "Have this, dear," she whispers, and I unwrap it from its crinkly clear paper and my mother's eyes suddenly flash at me, just for an instant, as I lift it to my mouth. The woman pats my shoulder, and the butterscotch dissolves while my mother keeps talking and smiling over the Bible, until she comes down the aisle again. She sits down, and I lean sighing against her warm stiff body. She is here now, everything is restored, the warm center of the world: my legs stick out in front of me on the chair, the white tights wrinkling over my knees, the round brown toes of my shoes. It is just she and I, and my father will be home when we get there. The walls recede again, and the other voices drone on all around as they have for as long as I can remember, three times a week in the Kingdom Hall.

Afterward, while she talks to people, I stand next to her leg, patting her soft skirt. I hold her hand all the way to the car.

The night is cold and black. The metal handle of the door is like ice, and the seat is cold and slidy. In the darkness, the cars and house roofs look like they've been dipped in silver. She doesn't start the car.

"Give me your M&M's," she says, looking straight ahead at the street, and I hand her the folded-over bag from the glove compartment, thinking she wants some. But she flips open the ashtray, dirty and full of my father's cigarette butts, and dumps in the little pieces. I hear their hard sides glittering against one another as they fall.

"That's for making Sister McLeod have to come over and give you a sweetie to keep you quiet," she says. Her face in the darkness is tight and bitter. She starts the car.

Heathrow Airport is the smell of sharp mint, of the Polo mints my father buys. One white circle for him, one for me, and then I may carry the roll in my pocket. When I hold his hand, he introduces me to people. I curtsey and ask them questions. When they say *how polite* or *what a charming child*, he ruffles my hair. The women laugh. In his office, I spin in his chair, draw on his memo pads. I pick up the phone when it's not ringing: "National Airlines. May I help you?" When he's busy, I can go play.

I stand near the ticket counters, the people lined up like a parade with their leather luggage, their brocade bags, all the different smells, the spicy odors and musk, the sharp scents of citrus, and the different colors of people's skin, gold, purply black, pale with copper freckles everywhere, and their costumes like in a drama at the assembly. The perfume of the Paris-bound wives in little suits, with their coiled platinum hair and handbags held on their wrists.

The sounds of their languages are ravishing. I stand listening by the velvet rope. Sometimes, after a while, I feel the excited shock when their words suddenly slip into clarity, and I can follow what they're saying: it's only English after all, pronounced differently.

I'm dazzled by the women in their saris, flame red with swirls of gold by the hem, purple with threads of green, their brown belly flesh burbling out. The red marks on their foreheads mystify me. *What for? What for?* No one at home can explain. The lazy ceiling fans in the waiting lounges, the packages bound with raffia, bulging open but not enough to see into. All the little shops. I get ten pence a week for my allowance. I am not to run, but sometimes I run. It is too thrilling to walk politely.

*   *   *

My mother takes me from our house in Ascot into Windsor to shop. Cut flowers mass out to the curb on the long road that spirals uphill. Gingerbread men sprawl, hot and grinning, on tin trays behind glass. Sometimes we take a tour of the castle.

In winter, I pause to look in windows filled with shimmering trees and dioramas: Father Christmases, crèches, elves, tiny people in old-fashioned clothes and top hats with their arms full of packages, the little ends of their scarves stuck stiffly in the air behind them, ice skaters twirling on mirrors, towers of ribboned packages.

"Stop it," she says, pulling me along. "That's pagan."

The Watchtower literature urges parents to teach their children to read early, so they can read the Bible and become loyal followers of Jehovah. My mother does; I sit on her lap, sounding out the words in a phonics book made to look like comics. Blue skies, snow, dogs, and children, all roundheaded like Charlie Brown. A pair of red mittens makes an *m*. When I am three, I read short passages from the Bible.

When I am five, I begin school in the first form. In the fall, I make the ominous journey, as every child must, across the school-yard to read aloud to Miss Chacey, the headmistress. Even her name is frightening, and her scalp shows pale between her crisped orange curls. But her voice when she speaks is friendly, and I read through the whole of the first primer and halfway through the second before she stops me.

"Very good," she says. "That's enough." She slides the jar across the desk to me and tells me to take two, instead of just one as my friends have gotten. I choose hard candies striped pink and yellow down their lengths and slip them into the pocket of my gray jumper, their cellophane twists crackling under my fingers as I walk back to class, uncertain but excited.

After the winter holidays, I am moved to the third form. I am in a different room with older children. Every day, each of us goes alone to Miss McIntyre's desk to read aloud; she moves us through the books as quickly as we can go. By the end of the year, I am on the twelfth reader. Next comes Louise Heath, with her curly dark hair and freckles, on the eighth.

I take ballet and love it. The tights, the tulle, the shining slippers. The other girls, their sweet fussing mothers, the wand for our recital that my mother helps me make from tin foil, cardboard, and a thin dowel. Onstage I become a fairy, a beautiful, twirling fairy, waving my Scotch-taped wand, changing things into better things.

Afterward, my mother is silent. The old Morris thrums as she drives us home in the dark. My father is away on business.

"Did you like it?" I finally ask. "Did I do all right?" She is silent. "Didn't you like the ballet?"

"Ballet?" she mutters. "You? More like the elephant walk." When we move to Miami later, when I am six, she will not reenroll me.

I cannot say why my mother chose derision and sarcasm. Perhaps she wanted to leave her mark on her children, and drawing blood was the only way she knew.

For her, we are failures, problems, embarrassments, things to beat with the wooden spoon she carries in her purse for that very purpose, or the back of a hairbrush, or the flat smacking sole of a sandal. I remember only one beating past the age of five and a few shaming slaps in public places, but I watched Tony beaten from the time he could toddle, and she's told laughing stories about taking me from a high chair to spank me.

I'm easily broken, and her scorn works like a bit and rein. She rolls her eyes when speaking of me to her friends. "She's so sensitive." She laughs. "All I have to do is cross my eyes, and she bursts into tears."

Getting lost is a gift my father gives me. Saturday mornings, we leave my mother sleeping and explore the English countryside.

"Which way?" he says at every intersection. I choose, and he turns. We drive until we are thoroughly lost. We stop at pubs for breakfast, for lunch. "Order anything you want," he says. We give each other bites of our food. We play the jukebox. We feed the ducks, laughing. Back in the car, we play the Beatles loud and sing along. I know to wait until there are no cars around to say, "Let's go to Windsor Castle," and he swerves wildly to the right, into the other lane, as if to drive directly there. I scream, laughing, begging him to get back where we belong. Then I say it again.

Each spring my family picnics in the fields around Kenilworth Castle. I love its red ruins. Cows chase us away.

We drive onto the hovercraft, through France, the Alps, the Black Forest. In the backseat, I put the tray table down and draw with my crayons. From my father's memo pads, I make books. "From the desk of . . . Lee Castro," the pages say, with the airline's logo, a smiling sun in profile. My books star animals of different species — bears, rabbits — having adventures or tea. I write along the bottom: *How do you do? Would you like cream? Hurry, run!* and staple the spines.

We stop to buy a cuckoo clock. On the street, a woman's voice cries, *"Liebchen! Liebchen!"* from above. Her pink face and arms emerge from red geraniums a story up, and handfuls of Pez sail down through the air to the sidewalk. I scramble to gather them up. My parents are ahead of me, hurrying to catch a taxi.

"Danke! Danke!" I cry, running backward toward the cab, waving my fists so she can see I've got them all. *"Danke!"* I squirm around in the seat and wave through the back window. The world is strange and generous.

"Children are emotional manipulators from the word go," my mother likes to say — to the aunts, to the Kingdom Hall sisters, to anyone who will listen.

She says it to my brother and me like a warning, like the first shot fired. She will not be taken in by our little ruses.

Babies are not to be coddled, particularly crying babies. If it's not wet or messed or hungry, she'll leave it in its crib to cry for hours. "You cried yourself to sleep every night of your life until you were three," she says, recollecting, annoyed. "Until you finally figured it out."

My stubbornness is legendary in the household: how, ignored, I would hold my breath until I fainted. They learned to catch me and put me somewhere soft, but otherwise they ignored it — the quickest way to break me of it.

She tells the stories with a note of triumph: she has won. She was not taken in.

All these incidents occur before my dawn of memory. I wake into consciousness a dutiful, obedient child. But curious.

My father's voice is beautiful. Deep, rich, with a soaring range. In high school, he had been onstage, acting, singing. Now he sings in the car: love songs, "The Kiss of Fire," Johnny Mathis, the lyrics of musicals. I sing with him, all the words to *Camelot*, *West Side Story*, *The Sound of Music*, *Oliver!*, *Oklahoma!*, and *Joseph and the Amazing Technicolor Dreamcoat*, which we see on the London stage and which my mother approves of the most, since it's a Bible story. I love the cleverness of lyrics, the humor, the way the words snap precisely into the length of the line. Sometimes we leave the eight-track player off and sing the whole show from memory. At home I sing "Norwegian Wood" over and over, swinging on my red plastic monkey seat under the tree.

My father loves make-believe as much as I do. (In a way, perhaps, so does my mother, always thrusting before me stories of a Paradise earth soon to come, lions and lambs lying together in the grass, families picnicking in the sun — a future on which my eyes should always be fixed, guiding my behavior toward godliness.) But my father loves fun, magic, the here and now. Each Thursday night,

I beg my mother to let me stay home from the meetings. Once in a while she gives in, drives off alone in the dark. Then my father and I sit, legs crossed, me in front with his arms around me, on the thick sheepskin rug by the fireplace.

"Hold on tight," he says, and it's a magic carpet, taking off from Heathrow. He describes all the things we're flying over. We lean from side to side as we swoop past Virginia Waters, the Taj Mahal, the palaces of Saint Petersburg, Niagara Falls. He points. "Oh, look!" he says, and describes it.

Sometimes on Friday afternoons, he rushes into the house, startling my mother, who doesn't expect him until eight, after I'm in bed. "I got a great deal!" he says. "Pack your bags. We're going to Paris!" And we go, just for the weekend. Amsterdam. Copenhagen.

In Cairo, we creep together up the dark, cramped passage inside a pyramid to the queen's tomb, wedging our heels against the bars of wood, while my mother, pregnant, waits outside. When we emerge to find her sweating and impatient, he disappears. "Where did your father run off to now?" she mutters. While our camels unfold upward to their feet, he gallops up garbed like a Bedouin and grabs her around the waist, and she laughs with her head thrown back.

She dines only at the Sheraton, carefully, thinking of the baby, but my father and I try food from all the vendors on the hot and crowded streets, and end our vacation in bed, attended by a doctor. But it was worth it, my father insists in a whisper: all the new flavors.

He takes me to London for my first movie, *Willy Wonka & the Chocolate Factory,* brings us to Disneyland, Universal Studios, Disney World, Tivoli Gardens, any carnival or fête that we can find in Britain or on the Continent. In hotel pools around the world, he teaches me to swim, humming "The Blue Danube" and whirling me softly in the water. Driving, we brake for maypoles. We tour every castle, get lost in palace mazes, ride from train stations in horse-drawn carriages instead of taking sensible taxis. I wave my gloved hand like the queen.

*   *   *

Make-believe. After I've grown up, during all the years we have trouble communicating, my father and I talk about movies. Once a week, when I call or he calls, if I do not have some achievement to report, we talk about movies we've seen, what we like and don't like. When he enrolls in college for the first time, at sixty, he takes a film course. For all our differences, our tastes in film are similar. Enthusiastic, we converse without strain.

In the year before his death, he begins going to Las Vegas. With friends, then with our stepmother, and then with friends again — compulsively so, our stepmother will tell us later. He doesn't gamble. He loves the spectacle, the make-believe of it all, and marvels at the inexpensive food.

When she finally serves him with divorce papers, he plans a trip for himself and Grey. We talk about it on the phone. They'll ride the roller coasters, eat at the buffets, see the fake Eiffel Tower, the fake Sphinx, the dancing fountains at the Bellagio.

It would not be my choice, but he sounds so hopeful, so excited. "He'll be dazzled," he says. He sends us "Grandpa Lee's Guide to Las Vegas," pages he's typed and bound of all the fun things to do with kids, and a videotape of attractions. We sit and watch the tape with Grey.

But they never make it.

At the funeral, our stepmother asks that all memorials be given to a cancer foundation. She works with cancer patients, has lost friends to cancer. It is a worthy cause, though one my father never spoke about.

My aunts, his sisters, quietly collect donations to put a brass plaque on one of the chairs in the auditorium at Key West High School, where once he acted and dreamed.

Libano Fabio Castro, 1939–2002.

Sarah the rag doll travels everywhere with us. My mother sews three matching dresses, white with tiny brown flowers: one for her, one for me, one for Sarah. Italian girls play with her by the Trevi Fountain in Rome, Dutch girls at Madurodam, Danish girls at Tivoli Gardens. In the black-and-white photographs I stand in my little plaid coat, sharing my doll and talking.

I make friends easily, my mother tells me later, though I cannot remember being bold. I chat up bobbies, chatter at the queen's guards at Buckingham Palace, who ignore me. I am fascinated by their faces that don't listen.

We fly free, so we fly. We stay in fancy hotels with my father's airline discount. He has flown alone with me since I was one; I find the records in my baby book, in my mother's hand, when I am thirty, the first time she lets me see it.

"My little thirty-two-year-old midget," he calls me, to the stewardesses who lean over to watch our in-flight checker games. They bring him drinks. I get to keep the tiny bottles of colored glass. At home, my dolls have their own bar. I play cocktail hour. "Mighty Mouth," he calls me when I chatter on, like Mighty Mouse, our favorite superhero.

On a sheet of company stationery, the lines of flight are mapped, a thick web sprawled over the United States: Miami, Chicago, New York, L.A. And one arc flung across white space, like a lone strand of spiderweb across a path. London. That was my father's job: to open the new station. The boy from Key West who learned English in school, the boy without a college education who pushed wheelchair passengers out to the plane and carried them up the stairs, before jetways. Spic labor. Who talked his way up to baggage, to ticket counter, to management. "Your father could sell ice to the Eskimos," says my mother, later, after the divorce, after what he'd sold her had melted away.

They were women he worked with, pretty women, younger women, women in some kind of trouble. My mother would find the inexplicable hotel receipt, confront him, forgive him when he wept and apologized and swore not to do it again. And then find another receipt.

I lie in her double bed in the dark as she cries and tells me. I am ten; we're in West Virginia, their last failed hope. My father has moved out. She likes me to come sleep with her. When I was little, when my father traveled on his business trips that weren't business trips, I would sleep in her bed. We would watch the car lights on the ceiling and feel calm.

Now I am floating above the bed in the darkness. She seems to be talking about my father: how funny, that she should be saying these things. My father, whom I adore. But she is crying. I come down. She is curled away from me, shaking the bed. I put my hand on her silky blue nightgown.

"Mama?" She jerks her shoulder away.

I am five, giving my first talk in the Kingdom Hall, pushing my memorized lines into the microphone, facing my mother, who sits next to me. We're demonstrating how a Bible study with a worldly person should transpire.

I've been onstage before to be the householder; that part's easy. You just ask questions that show you don't know The Truth. But this time I'm the one who's out in field service, the Witness. Conducting the Bible study is harder. You have to know the right scriptures to answer any questions, no matter what order they come in. But we've written out our parts and rehearsed at home, again and again. I am well dressed and shining clean for the occasion. I say my lines flawlessly, give looks of concern at the right times. Finally the householder agrees with everything I've said. It's the conclusion.

"Perhaps I can come back next week at this time to continue our discussion," I say.

"Yes, I'd like that very much." Her look is grateful; I am saving her from the confusions of her terrible sad life. Then she smiles, becoming my mother again.

We get down from the stage. Everyone claps, and we sit down together. She glows with pride, pats my knee. Everyone is proud of me. I am now a member of the Theocratic Ministry School. I can go out in service.

My mother wakes me in the mornings with a croon. "Wake up, my little buttercup. Rise and shine. Wake up, wake up," her gentle voice easing me from sleep. At night, once I'm trained docilely to let her go, she sings to me, *Shul, shul, shul a rul,* nonsense syllables that soothe, the skein of my mother's voice unspooling meaning — safety, love — without logic.

It's the kindness that breaks me. I'm trained, beaten. I hover for her approval, hoping. "Get out from underfoot," she snaps when I shadow her in the kitchen, trying to help with dinner.

When she is angry, I disappear. She can no longer see or hear me. It is a desperate invisibility. I struggle to think what she wants, what I have done to cross her. The shoes left in the living room? The unmade bed? A remark she would call smart? The smear of egg yolk on the counter? I rush to rectify. If I guess it right, I become real again. If not, the hours stretch like a swamp till my father comes home.

They stretched long for her, too, I see now.

Reading this, she would protest. She'd remind me of the book carnivals we had on the staircase, wedged next to each other as she read aloud every book I brought her, the two of us close, touching, happy together in one made-up world after another. Reading, she doesn't have to look at me: the inept dancer, impossible seamstress, splotchy painter, dangerous cook. With all my efforts, she grows impatient, snatches things out of my hands. "Here," does it right, slams them down in front of me.

Only at school, where the teachers are kind all day, do I excel. Even my mother cannot argue with the columns of neat A's and the comments in schoolteacher's script that say I am an excellent student, and so polite.

Reading this, she'd remind me of the days she let me stay home from school for no reason, just to keep her company. "Would you like a vacation?" she'd croon, before my eyes were even open.

Writing, I am liberated by one thing: that my mother approved of nothing I did or said. No matter what I put down here, it will be wrong, a kick in the teeth — a kick in the stomach, as she liked to say, from an ungrateful daughter. Whatever I do will be wrong. So I am free.

We must strive to be perfect as our Heavenly Father is perfect, she tells us. She is his judge on earth, as stern and unerring as God. There are a thousand ways to mess up. The road to heaven is narrow, and few are the ones who enter there.

Only when my son is born do I note that I can cook, sew, adequately clean a house. Only when I fall in love with a patient man do I learn that I have a gift for knocking them out of the park, that I can throw a football spinning through the air, control a soccer ball with the inner curve of my foot. "A natural athlete," he calls me, and I have to sit down, stunned for the years I called my body stupid.

The summer I am twenty-six, my mother comes to Texas, two months after Tony has moved down; she is hoping to see him. She hasn't since he turned eighteen. He doesn't want her to have his address, his phone number.

He refuses in the parking lot of the Lube King, where he changes oil all day, where I have come early to tell him it's okay, he doesn't have to see her if he doesn't want to, it's okay.

"Okay," he says. "Okay." He turns his back to the building. Tears slide down his cheeks. His face is streaked with oil and sweat. "I just can't, okay?"

I hug him on the hot cement, feel the sweat soak through the thick work shirt. It's a hundred and two degrees. "That's fine. That's no problem."

*　　*　　*

She's angry when I pick her up, mentions the price of the hotel room, how she can't think of a single earthly reason he would do such a thing. Surely it's only polite, given how much she's spent to get here. I drive. I keep her away from my house, my husband, my son. We drive to an amusing old town in the country, where we'll have things to look at and comment on: an antique rose emporium, an old church, a gazebo under oaks, a Civil War cemetery, artists' shops. We park on the side of the main road.

Heat and light bake us, bake the dusty streets. The only moving thing is a dog, sandy brown and collarless, wandering from awning-shade to awning-shade, panting, lapping at the few dirty puddles in the road. She's had a litter, maybe several: the pink line of her nipples sways beneath her. She looks tired, thirsty, hopeful. I wonder where her puppies are in this heat. She comes over to us, turns her mild brown eyes up to ours. I lean to pet her.

"That's disgusting," my mother says. "That's so revolting." I straighten up. She gestures at the dog's belly, vulnerable and exposed as having borne and nursed. "We shouldn't have to look at that thing. Someone should shoot it." She stamps her foot. "Shoo. Get."

The dog pads off. I look at my mother's pinched white mouth, the pouches of flesh under her chin, her eyes, her skin coated as always — except during the years my stepfather forbade it — with a layer of pancake makeup, the powder you wet a sponge to apply. My mother, whose slim, jaunty runway strut is long gone (even up the Kingdom Hall aisles, she'd jut her bosom proudly, swing her hips), whose double-D breasts now rest on a thick middle, whose black curls are cropped away to a straight gray helmet: my mother hates bodies. She hates her own body, my body as a child, the body of an innocent stray wandering dog. Something about the flesh offends her. And she hates female bodies most of all.

My baby book, strange document. White covers touched with gold, titled *Our Baby's Keepsake*, it looks normal, and the inside is carefully filled in my mother's neat hand, the dutiful hand of an adoring mother, circa late sixties.

Day of Arrival. Baby is a *girl* born on the *ninth* day of *October, 1967,* at *10–11* o'clock. News Headlines of the Day: *Democrats Pick Chicago as Site for Convention.* Named for: *Our happiness.* A little envelope: *Bangs cut by Mama on Feb. 18, 1969.* Baby's First Home, *12710 SW 84 Ave. Road — Miami, Florida,* with a black-and-white photograph of a Florida-style bungalow, with its carport, flat lawn bisected by a walk, metal shades hovering over the windows, the fronds of a palm hanging into the corner of the shot.

My naps, vaccines, illnesses, and baby gifts are neatly recorded. But there are strange slippages, the whole document a mélange of Jehovah's Witness orthodoxy, airline travel (the trips recorded with just the shorthand a former stewardess would use: *March 9–Apr 5 — LON-NYC-MIA-ORD-LON; Jan 5 — MIA-SNN-PIK-LON*), and my affection for my father.

Baby's Favorites.

0–6 Months — games with her Daddy

6 Months — Loves to play peek-a-boo mostly with damp washcloth. Joy loves the water — to swim, bathe, or just look at.

12 Months — Loves peek-a-boo games — still likes to rough house with her daddy.

18 Months — Plays dolls and rough with Daddy. Any kind of verse appeals and must be repeated again & again. All music thrills her. She dances and sings. Sings at the Hall, too!

On the page "Baby's 1st Birthday," the printed heading "How the Birthday Was Celebrated" is struck through with blue ink. *Joy at age one was a delight — plays well and is always happy unless some specific reason. Loves dolls, music, books. Joy and* ~~Lee~~*Daddy go out alone every Saturday morning for breakfast and to the park to feed the ducks. Sleeps well and eats anything and everything. She really is the perfect child.*

2nd Birthday. ~~How the Birthday Was Celebrated~~. *By age two Joy* has a vocabulary to equal any situation. She recites Robert Louis Stevenson's "Time to Rise," "The Swing," and "Singing Time," by Rose Tyleman.

She counts to 15 usually in order though not always. Can identify a circle, square, triangle and hexagon. Loves riding down the "Big Slide" on burlap sacks with her daddy and feeding the ducks, going to the park.

Enjoys field service twice a week and plays at going to the Kingdom Hall and door-to-door. Calls us Dad and Mom — and says, "We're a whole family and we love each other."

"Why?" is a very popular question! Says her prayer each nap time and bedtime. "Thank you Jehovah for a good day, I love Jehovah and Jesus. Amen." Can identify several countries in the yearbook and enjoys hearing the daily text and "feriences" (experiences) at lunch each day.

Favorite expressions: "I don't believe it!" "Knock it off," "What happened?" Knows stories of Adam & Eve, Noah, Jericho, Jonah and Moses who was "dopted by the queen." Eats well, sleeps well, plays well.

Early ~~Christmases~~ Assemblies.

1968 June 7, 8, & 9 — slept or ate through most sessions

1969 January 9, 10, 11 Joy attended Friday night and was fussy — Sat. stayed home, but Sunday was very good.

July 21–27 Peace on Earth Assembly — White Sox Park, Chicago, Illinois — Joy attended all sessions with Mom & Dad except Saturday night. Behaved well and enjoyed the fine talks, songs, and association.

1970 June 19–21 — Dorking, Surrey assembly — rode on the coach to all meetings — out in service on Sat morning with the Thornes. Joy made friends with all the children.

August 6–9 — Twickenham assembly — made most of the talks but rain, etc prevented all. Enjoyed and Joy behaved well.

The "Memorable Holidays" page — Valentine's Day, Easter, Halloween, and Others — is blank.

From birth, then, I am immersed in what Jehovah's Witnesses call The Truth: the meetings, the assemblies thronged with tens of thousands of believers, the songs, the door-to-door preaching, the doctrines, the prayers.

Assemblies are marathons of truth, two- or five- or seven-day meetings in large venues — stadiums or racetracks. Circuit assemblies, district assemblies, international assemblies. When the talks are going on, we must be in our seats, paying attention, but there are breaks. There are blue tickets for lunch, like a carnival. There's a festive air. Children can wander off, get lost. It's all brothers and sisters. There's a safe sense of chaos.

Each morning a gorgeous stage is set up, away from the main platform. I stare at it all through the overseers' talks, wondering what the drama will be like. I long to be in a drama. I want to wear the simple raiment of the Israelites and say my lines in a solemn godly tone. But Canaanites have more fun. They wear prettier clothes and get to wave their tambourines, dancing wildly to idols. "You have to *become* your character," I've heard my father say, and I wonder what those brothers and sisters feel inside their Canaanite costumes, and if Jehovah minds.

In the baby book, my mother comments, too, upon my appetite, with an indecipherable mixture of pride and unease:

> 0–6 mos   *eats everything in sight*
>
> *Loves <u>Ice Cream</u>*

At six months refused baby food and went to table food — soup for lunch and whatever Mommy and Daddy were having for supper.

> 12 mos.   *Eats anything that doesn't eat her first.*
>
> 18 mos.   *Loves avocadoes and must have noodle-ohs for lunch <u>everyday</u>*

My father loves to see children eat, as does his mother, Nanny. A good appetite means a healthy child, she tells us when we visit her in Key West. My father breaks off small lumps of avocado, banana, and feeds them to me with his fingers, eager, his eyes crinkling with delight. But my mother is ambivalent.

August 1971 LON-CPH-LON — As usual enjoyed Tivoli Gardens —
also went to Backen. As usual she and her daddy devoured hot dogs
incessantly.

My mother and I fly alone from England to Chicago, where her
family lives. I am small, just tall enough to open by myself the drawer
my aunt has pointed out to me, a drawer full of candy, all kinds.
"Help yourself," she says. "Take as much as you want."

All afternoon and evening the grown-ups talk in the other
room, laughing together on the brightly lit couches. I'm the only
child there. We stay late, past my bedtime, but no one notices. I
wander through the house alone, slipping back into the darkened
kitchen for more candy when I'm bored.

The next day, at my grandmother's house, my mother crouches
and grabs my shoulders.

"Are you proud of yourself?" she says. I try to think of what I've
done. "That was your aunt Sue on the phone. She wanted to know if
you were all right."

"I'm fine," I say, confused, and her face gets angrier.

"She wanted to know if you were *all right,* young lady, because
she couldn't see how anyone could eat so much candy without getting sick." She shakes me. "Don't you ever do that again. Do you hear
me? Don't you *ever* embarrass me like that. Behaving like a little pig."
Her face is close to mine; the black lines around her eyes are blurry
and uneven and the skin under them is raw pink. Her tear ducts glis-
ten yellow, like pus. "You should be ashamed of yourself," she says finally, letting go and straightening up. Her words fall down to me at
their usual volume. "You're disgusting. Get out of my sight."

Ascot Heath Infant School, Fernbank Road, Ascot, Berkshire.
Interests. Likes to draw, sing, dance, swim. In fact Joy does every-
thing wholeheartedly and with gusto.

Special Events. *Joy was the Pussy Cat for the school entertainment — wore black tights and a black headband with pointed ears.*

The entries end when I am five. My mother and father sit me down in their bedroom, all of us on the silky bedspread with its big purple flowers. Soon, they tell me, I will have a new little brother or sister. A baby! A new little brother or sister of my very own, to take care of and hold and love. They have gone to special doctors so that Mommy could get pregnant. This one won't be adopted. I'll get to watch her tummy grow. They ask if I have any questions. I rub the bedspread with my fingers.

"Can I have a pony instead?"

They laugh. This is hilarious. They must tell their friends.

"No, really," I say, "I'd rather have a pony," and their faces settle. They explain. They repeat it: " 'Can I have a pony?' " and laugh, and I laugh, too.

But when my brother comes, chinless and red-faced, I hold him on my lap until my legs fall asleep. His black thatch falls away and he grows shining gold hair, soft smooth locks of it to pet, and he smiles. I read him my favorite books, Beatrix Potter, *The Little Engine That Could.* I carry his sweet, dense weight around the house and give him his bottle, and later I spoon him his food. I get to put his shirt on and button up his little jackets.

When he is nine months old, we leave England.

4

On the 747, I sit upstairs in the lounge alone. It's dark and empty, wrapped in glass. I watch stars in the blackness. After four years, my father's position in London has ended. We're moving back to Miami, a home I can't remember.

My mother trips on the spiral staircase, carrying my brother, and breaks her toe. It wouldn't have happened, she says, if my father had been helping, instead of carrying on with that stewardess.

When Tony starts to toddle, I hold his hand and go everywhere with him to make sure he doesn't get into anything or hurt himself. He has a cheery little grin. I talk to him and tell him stories, and he follows me like a duckling. I do silly things just to hear his gurgly chuckle.

Later, when he's one and a half, two, and my mother starts to beat him, I hate her. I hold him on my lap afterward, hiding us in my room.

"She loves you," I whisper. "She doesn't mean to hurt you." I pet his smooth hair as he shivers.

When he's better, we play rabbits together, our knees sliding on the wooden floors, hopping under furniture to get away from Mr. McGregor and his sack.

At the Kingdom Hall in Kendall, he leans out into the aisle, a wiggly child. We are to sit perfectly still for two hours each Sunday morning and Thursday night, and another hour Tuesday evening. He can't do it.

"Please, Jehovah, make it end," he yells plaintively, hanging half his body into the aisle, and brothers and sisters titter around us.

My mother grabs him by the arm and marches him out. He toddles along next to her, waving to everyone in the rows. "Bye," he says, happy, thinking he sees freedom. "Bye." I turn to look; no one meets his eyes or laughs now. And then they're outside, and we can hear the fall of the object on his legs, and his screams. When they come back his face is red and wet, and his little legs are red, and she shoves him into the seat between us. She stares fiercely, chin high, at the talking brother. Where she cannot see, I slip my hand around my brother's and squeeze. He clings on, sniffling.

Over and over, he wiggles just too much for her to tolerate. At meeting after meeting, the two of them march down the aisle as I sit alone. If she has forgotten the wooden spoon or hairbrush, it's all right. There are trees, some with all the twigs stripped off. All the parents use them.

I don't know how to save him. I try sitting between them so she can see less, but she makes us move back.

"I've never been so exasperated in my life," my mother says to him in the car one day on the way home. "When are you going to learn? I don't know if you're really this stubborn, or just plain stupid."

"He's just little."

"What did you say to me?" She looks away from the road, her brows arched. "What did you say?"

"I said, he's just little."

"Just who do you think you are?" I hate it when she says this. There's no good answer. Whatever I say makes her mad. "Well, young lady? Who do you think you are?"

"Joy Elizabeth Castro."

"Don't you get smart with me."

"Why do you have to spank him all the time? He's just little."

"You're not too old for a spanking yourself. You understand me?"

"Well, how would *you* like one?"

The car veers over on the side of the road and jerks to a stop, kicking up gravel. She turns to me, her face dark with blood under the makeup. "What did you say to me?"

"I just mean, you wouldn't *like* getting spanked every time you made a mistake. Even if you deserved it." I backpedal, my tone freshly humble. "I didn't mean you *ought* to get a spanking. I just mean, you can understand how he feels, if you think about it."

"Hmm. Well," she says. She sighs. Her chin tilts up so her eyes point at the sky. "Foolishness is tied up with the heart of a boy," she quotes, "and the rod of discipline is what will remove it from him." She shifts into gear and pulls back on the road. Glances down at me, her lips pursed in that holy way. "Proverbs 22:15."

"*Far* from him," I quote. She sighs again.

I cannot recall being hauled out of the Kingdom Hall and beaten. It would have been the Kingdom Hall in England, but in my earliest memories there, I sit perfectly still next to my mother, my Bible in my lap, looking up the scriptures when the brothers refer to them, because I know the books of the Bible in order, by heart. What a little angel, the other sisters say. Such a little lamb.

I remember only one beating, but it happened at home, my mother's hands smacking down on my legs, thighs, face, my arms over my head, her hands thwacking down everywhere and her face like a white mask, lipless with fury.

I am six, we have just moved back to Florida, and we live in a tiny apartment — so small that Tony's nursery is the closet — in a complex like a maze. All the buildings are identical, the same bland tan, the winding paths between them just alike, all the dark bushes trimmed the same shape, indistinguishable.

The first day of school, she walks me to the bus stop, as she had walked me to school each day in England. The second morning, she sends me out alone. I leave with my lunchbox in the dark. Shadows loom everywhere. Everything looks alike, and I can't tell which way to turn. I get lost and run home crying.

When she opens the door, she's on the phone. She gestures me into my room, up onto my bed, the long cord swinging behind her. She leaves, shutting the door. For a long time I can hear her voice, upset, rising and falling. And then she is in my room, she is on me, her hands are smacking everywhere.

The apartment complex has a pool, and my father takes me swimming. He reclines in a deck chair in the sun, talking with a friend of his, a man I do not know. I get out and stand next to him, dripping.

"Daddy. Daddy." They keep talking. "Daddy."

"What is it?"

"I have to pee."

"Okay, go pee."

"I'm going back to the apartment."

"Can't you use the clubhouse?"

"It's closed."

"Oh, okay. Tell Mommy hello."

"Okay." I go home, pee, get some juice and drink it while I watch my mother put Tony down for a nap. The little animals turn in a circle above him, and the tinkling music gets slower and slower. The smooth balls of his closed eyelids wiggle.

When I come back, the two men are standing at the edge of the pool, leaning over, with their backs to me.

"What's in there?" I ask.

My father whirls. "Jesus Christ!" he says. "Where the hell have you been?"

He's never looked like this before, never talked in that voice, angry, afraid. I start to cry.

"At home. With Mommy." His face is furious, and the other man is staring at me. My voice lifts, frightened. "I was peeing," I say, desperate.

"Jesus. You can't just run off like that." He crouches down and takes my shoulders in his hands. "Do you understand?"

I nod. He pulls me close against him.

"Jesus, honey. You scared the hell out of me."

"She's okay," the other man says.

"Promise me you'll never do that again." My father's voice has a strangled sound. "Do you hear? Promise me."

I promise.

My father shoots himself in daylight, in public, in his parked car. Police surround him.

He is right-handed. The bullet enters his right temple and exits (more or less) his left, shattering the driver's side window. The front-page photo shows the cops with their guns drawn: when the window shatters, they think he's shooting at them. But he's already dead.

He is sixty-two. He is retiring. My stepmother has served him with divorce papers one month ago; it's the deadline for his response. The divorce — that's what the two-page, typed, furious, stunningly lucid suicide note blames. My brother and I are included in the *cc:* line. Meticulous.

My father never owned a handgun in his life. A deer rifle, briefly, but he gave it up once he'd seen a buck die. He was always a gentle man. He couldn't spank us, never yelled.

We arrive for the funeral, sleep two nights in his home, the house I lived in for two years after I ran away from my mother and stepfather, where my brother lived for nine. Tony finds the gun safe in the dining room cupboard. The date and serial number are neatly recorded in his handwriting on the booklet's last page, as required. He'd owned it for exactly a month. Meticulous.

He would stand at the table in the post office, opening his mail, writing checks for the bills, stamping, sealing, mailing them. He checked the *No* box for the several music clubs he joined over the years; no CDs arrived by accident. He threw the junk mail in the trash and left clean-handed.

I am a sloppy daughter. I don't cook. I can read a whole novel in a messy room, unperturbed. Papers litter my desk at work. At home, mail stacks up on the piano.

When I am in college, my father calls.

"I *have* emotions," he says.

"Okay." I'm bewildered. It might be a joke.

"I do," he insists.

"Okay, fine."

"That time you said I didn't feel anything? That I just manage everyone? Well, I feel things."

"Okay," I say. "I'm sorry." I can't remember what he's talking about.

"You were angry about something? You were crying? You still lived at home." Four years ago. He pauses. "But I do. I was driving on the highway and listening to a Johnny Mathis song, and it made me feel like crying. So I did," he says. "I cried a few tears on I-79."

In adolescence, young adulthood, I believe my father is a wall. A rock, my brother calls him: dependable, solid. *Same stuff,* I mutter.

As it turns out, he's neither. And he's gone, gone over a breakup like a stupid, stupid high school boy who wanders out into the snow with a shotgun when his girlfriend likes somebody else.

Water pulls me, draws me down to it. Barbados, Long Beach, the shore of Lake Superior. I leave the conference, my briefcase, my name badge, and let the water pull me toward its edge. Facedown I lie on the hot rocks, the hot sand, silent, just at the brim-point of the arriving waves, their slosh and thump in my ears. The pulse beats in my naked ankle like a fawn, like a reply.

Literary critics have a field day with water, with its symbolism. We love its fluidity. *Sex,* we say easily, as if we know. Or *baptism, life, renewal.* Or *death.*

Swimming was what I did with my father. On beaches and in hotel pools, we would wave to my mother arranged on her towel; in the water, my body is sleek, effortless, and hidden from her. The liquid sliding and the rhythm of my own motions feel beautiful; it's a secret I keep from her critical eye. My father likes water, too. As a little boy, he leaped from the Key West docks into twenty feet of water, plunged recklessly into a dark unknown. He did not lack for courage. It's how he learned to swim.

The night he dies, I gulp it out in private, to my husband alone, as we're getting ready for bed. *I want to be with my father.* Later, we don't speak of it. I never refer to it, my admission, a moment of weakness; I don't want to scare anyone. But on walks, I learn to avoid busy stretches of highway, because my muscles twitch when semis approach, as though they can feel in their imagination what my good dutiful mind won't let me think: the bludgeoning and blessed instant peace.

After his death, I swim too far in a lake in Bellingham, vacationing with my family, happy, forgetting grief for a while, lying on my back alone and looking at the clouds. And then remembering, and seeing how far I am from shore, from any other person, the lake's pull hitting me all at once like gravity, a sinister promise of release. I hang there, feeling it. And then cut swiftly back through the dark water toward my husband and Grey, where they're laughing together on the raft, in the sun.

Now when I travel, I confine myself to the shallows, the shore. After a mindless while at the edge, I pin my name badge carefully back on and reenter my life.

*   *   *

"These are litchi nuts," the pretty woman says, bending down to show me one.

"It doesn't look like a nut."

"No, you're right. More like a fruit, or a berry." She breaks it, pushing open its red skin and spreading the white translucent flesh inside. She pats my head, smiles at my father. "Well, isn't she bright?" she says.

We are in Florida, not far from our house. The woman's yard is large and treed, like a park, but thickly grown over with plants and weeds. There's a high fence around it; I can hear the muffled sounds of cars.

"Now see how many you can find," my father says. It will be a game, they tell me. The woman smiles as she hands me a Tupperware bowl. They head toward her house.

I wander, picking, sweating. The sun is so hot and bright that the grass and leaves look yellow. The buzz of insects rises and falls. The litchi nuts are sweet. They have a cool taste, even though they are not cool. I sit, drowsy, on a rock, the bowl full, until my father emerges. On the way home, he laughs and plays the music loud. We never visit there again.

In Miami, my mother takes me to the Johnsons' house, which is small and hot and crowded with children, all sizes. My mother and Sister Johnson sit at the kitchen table talking, their Bibles open in front of them, while the big kids set up the Slip'N Slide with the hose in the backyard. All afternoon we laugh and scream, running and leaping on its long wet stretch of yellow.

"I am so glad to be back among our black brothers and sisters again," my mother says, driving home. "There just weren't any in the congregation in Surrey."

I am seven. At the Kingdom Hall in Kendall, the brother on the platform announces that Lee Castro is disfellowshipped, for smoking.

This is not a public reproof, which would mean that the Witness is repentant and wants to remain in the flock. It's a disfellowshipping, a full excommunication. He says it in a serious manner, a warning way, his lips close to the metal microphone, his eyes intent upon us. People turn in their seats to look at us. Their faces are sad, pitying. Next to me, my mother is rigid, staring straight ahead. She nods slightly, as if to acknowledge their concern. My brother squirms in his seat.

But nothing really changes. When we come home from the meetings at noon on Sundays, our father still makes us runny-centered eggs and bacon and asks how everything went. He still takes us places: the Monkey Jungle, the Parrot Jungle, the Serpentarium, the Seaquarium. He still can make our mother laugh. The brothers and sisters still chat politely with him when he's with us somewhere. He's still Daddy.

Brothers can face the congregation and talk to us directly, make eye contact, because Paul wrote to the Ephesians that men are the head of the household. They're allowed to tell us what to do. Sisters can only suggest by demonstrating, setting a good example without commanding anyone. If by some emergency there aren't any brothers around, sisters can wear a headscarf, to show they know their place, and lead the meeting. If they don't have a scarf, they can use a hanky.

It is a complicated hierarchy, with sisters at the bottom. Above them are brothers, and above the whole congregation is the small group of elders. Above the elders, there is the circuit overseer, and, above him, the district overseer, who visits every now and then with his wife. (Not until college will I learn that *overseer* was the word for the man who watched and disciplined slaves. When I am a child, it's a natural word to me: the sound still means the thing.)

The sisters' talks are more interesting. They face each other. It's like a little play or story. They pretend to be characters. The brother just stands at the podium and blah blah, tells us what to do.

I've learned to point my face neatly toward him, as if transfixed, but my eyes are on my lap, where my Bible lies open to the Song of Solomon. *Bind me as a seal upon your heart, as a seal upon your arm, for love is as strong as death is* —. It's the cheap green edition, the one all the children have, and I long for a grown-up Bible, one with black flexible covers textured like leather, with curved corners and gold gilt edging around the pages and a tightly woven black bookmark like a ribbon. I carry my mother's around the house, pretending.

I get one when I'm eleven, when I'm first allowed to wear high heels and panty hose to the meetings.

Like every community, we have our jargon. Preaching is called going door-to-door, or going out in service — the former like a salesman, the latter like a maid. After we've joined the ministry school and started going out in service, we are called publishers. To go door-to-door for a hundred hours a month is to pioneer. Sixty hours a month is auxiliary pioneering. Ordinary Witnesses try to auxiliary pioneer when they can. Some Witnesses, usually young adults without spouses or children, pioneer full-time, for even more hours. They're called special pioneers, and the other Witnesses do what they can to support their efforts: meals, money, the use of a guest room.

We meet in fine new structures designed to be Kingdom Halls, built by brothers while sisters bring potato salad and tea. We meet in old converted buildings. But it's always a Kingdom Hall; it always has a platform, podium, and neat rows of uncomfortable chairs in which we must sit still.

We cannot say *God* or *Jesus* in an exclamation, and we cannot say *gosh* or *golly* or *gee* or *gee whiz,* because these are forms of those words. We cannot wish someone *good luck* because there is no such thing as luck, only Jehovah's will and the temptations of Satan the Devil.

The most crucial rule of all is that we must always, always tell the truth, no matter what the consequences are, for we must model ourselves on Jehovah, and it is impossible for him to lie. We cannot say *shut up* because it is rude.

"Cheese and crackers, got all muddy," my father says some-times, in a way that sounds like *Jesus Christ, God almighty.* My mother glares at him. Sometimes he says, "Balzac," resting long on the first syllable.

It's difficult to reconstruct what it must have meant to me, at five years old or nine or fourteen: the hours of irritation and hostility from strangers every week as we mounted their front steps — the doors slammed, the voices lifted in anger, as I did what I'd been trained from birth to do, what I'd been taught was right and good. It's difficult to conceptualize what it all made me come to believe about the world and my place in it.

"They're so manipulative," an academic, a new acquaintance, says at a dinner one night. It's a professional dinner for writers and scholars, so no one at the table knows my background: it's not something I bring up. Conversation has drifted from telemarketers to religious zealots. "Anything you say, they make a way in, a way to try to convince you. I mean, I try to be polite. But they just won't take no for an answer." Everyone agrees. They're so annoying.

I agree, too. I've tried to get them to leave. "I'm an apostate," I finally say, and they back away, eyes wide, stuffing tracts hurriedly back in their book bags.

But I remember the hours of practice, at home with my mother, onstage at the Kingdom Hall giving talks, listening to those given by others, and the tension at the doors of strangers, how I was faulted later if I let an opportunity slip. The householder's mind and heart were reachable, if you could only remember all the answers, all the scriptures for any objection, all the automatic right replies. That was the purpose of the Theocratic Ministry School, all the talks on Thursday nights — to train us. If I went to a door and left with that *Watchtower* and *Awake!* still in my hand, the failure was probably mine. Only if I had done everything exactly right, lobbing back the right scriptures no matter how the householders responded, then I could rejoice and take comfort, for they were simply rocky soil, and I had been persecuted in Jehovah's name. But only then.

As a child going door-to-door with my mother or another Kingdom Hall sister or, later, with my stepfather, I place the magazines with householders, collect their dimes for Jehovah. I place small pink books, *Listening to the Great Teacher,* with my classmates. (Fifteen years later, in college, I'll find a copy at the Goodwill and spend the evening drinking Shiner with my friend Heather, passing the book back and forth to read passages aloud, laughing hysterically. "Satan the Devil" is the phrase that slays her. "Satan *the Devil,*" she keeps repeating. "Like, Satan who else?")

In sixth grade, I place fourteen red youth books with kids in my class. With its cautionary chapters on dating, drinking, drugs, and — the one I read and reread —"Masturbation and Homosexuality," it's an easy sell. Yawning with nervousness, I go onstage at a circuit assembly in Pittsburgh, describing my triumph for Jehovah to hundreds of clapping Witnesses.

But only a few times do I place the most important book, the one we study with new converts before they can be baptized in The Truth. A small blue book that goes for a quarter, *The Truth that Leads to Eternal Life* has on its cover an open book surrounded by symmetrical rays of light. The truth book, we call it, as we call *Listening to the Great Teacher* the great teacher book, or *Paradise Regained* the paradise book.

The truth book, it seems to me, is more boring than the books for kids: no stories, few pictures. But at eleven or twelve, I read it. It's time. I've seen most of my friends baptized, stepping down into the special pool in their swimsuits, holding their noses, getting dunked backward by a brother robed in white. It's a chance to check out the boys' bodies. Soon it will be my turn.

The bulk of the truth book lays out several principles by which anyone can identify the one true religion. It states the principles — such as the true religion worships the only true God, Jehovah, and its followers call him by his right name; and the true religion does not believe in Christendom's false teachings about the eternal soul, the Trinity, or torment in hell — supports them with Bible verses, and then points out that only Jehovah's Witnesses fulfill them.

I'm mystified. I ask my mom about it on the way home from the Kingdom Hall one Sunday afternoon.

"How can you tell the true religion?" I start.

She ticks off the principles, never pulling her eyes from the road. "You know that."

"Okay, but how can you know that the principles are right?"

She looks at me, opens and shuts her mouth. "They're right because they're in the truth book. They're right because the Bible says so."

"I know. But people picked the principles. They *made up* the principles, and then picked the scriptures to go with them." I'm excited. I'm onto something. "What if they're wrong?" I fiddle with the corner of my book bag.

"The brothers at Bethel are guided by Jehovah. They're not wrong."

"But they tell you all the marks of the true religion, and then it turns out to be *their* religion. Anybody could do that." I pull out a *Watchtower* and start slapping it on the dashboard. "*I* could do that." Slap, slap. "I could say, 'The only true religion says peanut butter is evil,' and then I could find scriptures that could be *interpreted* that way, and then make up a religion that really thinks peanut butter is evil, and then—"

Her hand whips out, snatches the magazine, throws it in my lap. "That's enough, young lady. That's disrespectful."

"I'm just asking."

"Yeah, well, you're just a little smart aleck, you know that?"

"No, I'm smart." I fold my arms. Teachers say so.

"No, you're a smart aleck. There's a difference."

"No, I'm smart." I mimic her tone. "There's a difference." Her hand darts out again but stops before it hits my leg. There's a long pause as she pulls her hand back to the wheel. "Jehovah gave me a brain. I guess he wants me to use it."

"That's just about enough," she snaps. "I don't want to hear another word out of you until we're home." She glances over. "Do you hear me? Not a word."

She drives. I stare out the window. My brother sleeps in the backseat. It's a forty-five-minute trip to our house. We wind through the mountains. After a while, she says in a milder tone, "The true religion is based on faith, and if you don't have the faith to know it, maybe you'd better take it up with Jehovah. In prayer."

I say nothing.

"Don't you think?"

I've been reading the Great Brain books in order, and I've decided that I have a lot in common with Tom Fitzgerald, old T.D., who outwits the doltish grown-ups under whose rule he must still live.

"Well, young lady? Are you going to answer me?"

"You told me not to say anything till we got home. I mean, if you want me to break your own rules—"

An exasperated hiss escapes her, and she grabs the steering wheel at ten and two.

I hadn't heard of Milton yet and didn't know the word *tautology*. I wouldn't until college. But I felt a swell of happy power. In my bones, I suddenly felt there were other kinds of heroes than the obedient ones in *Listening to the Great Teacher* who shunned the long-haired boys, or the ones in the ugly peach-colored paradise book with its bas-relief cover of fully clothed modern people in Eden. Heroes, I realized, could rise up, disobedient, their tongues full of questions, instead of just lying there to wait like boring Isaac for the knife.

5

My father loves to play with words. I am five. Hiking at Virginia Waters, we see starry splotches of green and gray on the rocks.

"It's lichen," says my mother, the obliging straight man, beginning their routine.

"Liken to what?"

"Liken to lichen." And off they go, like the Marx brothers on TV.

In the empty house after he dies, there are books of puns, the origins of common expressions, the genesis of words now defunct. He loved a bad pun; off-color was best. If you said the word "sticker," he'd say, "You stick 'er, you brought 'er to the party." We grew up groaning.

He prized English, played with English, mastered it to show he could.

"C-A-T," he sounded out phonetically the first day of school, his pronunciations the pronunciations of the Spanish alphabet, and the children laughed. Fifty years later, he remembers the shame, laughs too.

Except for the four years that we'll live in genuine poverty with our mother and then with our stepfather, our family is lower middle class, a status lacking in much glamour. But because of my father's work with the airlines, we enjoy the odd accoutrements of wealth: free travel, discounted hotels, cheap tickets to expensive places. For the four years we live in England, from 1969 to 1973, because of his paycheck circumstances — British salary, American taxes — we live well. My mother takes a Cordon Bleu cooking course, my father drives a secondhand Jaguar, and their closet holds gowns and tuxedos for parties for his work. A small-town boy without a college education, my father meets with ambassadors to make decisions about international air travel, tariffs, hijackings, the strikes of air traffic controllers. He has a jewelry box divided into little sections for his cuff links, and he lets me stomp squeakily around the room in his black patent leather shoes while he dresses. At the Russian embassy, he is offered a case of vodka by a foreign aide.

As a five-year-old, I know all about James Bond, because my father talks about him. It is the life he is trying to lead. In college, I learn the word *assimilation* and realize it is his story.

Lou, Lettie, Lee. Only Aunt Linda's name remains intact, un-Anglicized, acceptable in its original form. Lourdes, Leticia, Libano — after Mount Lebanon, which Papi saw as a young man before his fortunes brought him west across the ocean, into the arms of the printer's daughter. Mount Lebanon, the most beautiful sight he'd ever seen. Libano. Powerful, noble, verdant. A fitting name for a son.

At fifteen, he makes love for the first time, to a beautiful Cuban girl named Sonia, whose one arm is withered from polio. Bold for thirteen, she climbs onto his lap, leaves her first-time blood on his white shorts. They pledge themselves to each other. He tugs his shirttails down, buys a chocolate cone on the way home and rubs the ice cream on his crotch to conceal the stain, so his mother will not know.

For three years, my father and Sonia make love. He stars in plays at the high school, and she comes to watch and applaud him. He is

Cyrano, an irony they laugh about, because my father is so handsome, like Desi Arnaz on TV, only younger.

Obediently he works in the print shop with his father and brother Mario. But he will not be a boy forever. What does he care about setting type for hours, the tiny letters meticulously placed? What does he care for the Spanish-language newspaper his family has published for generations, the advice column for Cuban housewives his grandmother wrote? Who cares about business cards for businesses that only reach other Conchs? The world is a wider world, he knows — wider than this three-mile spit of sand, for sure — and its language is not Spanish.

His parents' wedding gift had been a trip around the island in the island's first automobile, owned by the doctor. Later, they would fly to Cuba to visit Nanny's people. Papi never returned to Spain, and none of his thirteen brothers and sisters came to visit him. He never saw again the green hills of Galicia, where he'd herded sheep as a boy, never again saw Villalba, the village of his birth, or the farm where his family had grown grapes, barley, wheat, pears. His wealthy uncle had seen promise, plucked young Feliciano up and taken him to Havana, where he raised him as his own son. At fourteen, Papi was dressed as a gentleman and sent to a Jesuit school in Rome; he told my father stories of playing tag on the rooftop amid the old statues. At nineteen, finished with his formal education, he saw Europe, the Mediterranean, and crossed to Cuba, where his uncle had the bad grace to die — suddenly, unexpectedly, and with no provision for his favorite nephew.

In Tampa, he worked at the magazine *La Bohemia* for fifteen dollars a month before taking his baritone and fine elocution to a cigar factory in Key West, where he read literature and the news in Spanish to nimble-fingered men. He was introduced to the island's editor, Juan Rolo, who printed the Spanish newspaper, who did all the printing jobs for the Cuban businesses, whose daughter Sofia was beautiful, dark-eyed, young. After they'd married, after she'd borne a daughter, Argentina, who lived long enough only to be named and buried, and a son, my uncle Mario, and the stillborn baby that killed her, the family gave him a younger daughter to keep his house and make more babies: Virginia, my grandmother. We called her Nanny.

Papi wrote a book of poems, printed it on the press. *Lágrimas y Flores.* Tears and flowers. I translated a few verses in college. It was boring, wordy, Victorian in its protestations. I quit.

My father — not great, fat, kind Uncle Mario dying of cancer, his pockets full of candy — was the one who could make the print shop a going concern, keep printed Spanish alive on the island. The girls hadn't been trained.

But to succeed means to leave home. It was the story my grandfather's own life told: You are the one with the blaze in your eye, the one with the quick, assured manner. You are the one they recognize, choose, invite into new worlds, warm houses full of books and the laughter of women.

Papi was too proud to plead. My father left for Miami at eighteen, knowing and not knowing he was breaking the heart of an old stag.

Later I learn Papi paid the thousand dollars for my parents to adopt me. Was he embarrassed that his son had not produced a child, eager to shield him from shame? I know he was pleased that the lawyer promised a Latino infant. With black-brown eyes, dark hair, and fair skin, I look, as a baby, like his own girls had as children.

On the way from the hospital, my father pulls the car off the road —"crying with joy," he says to my mother, and I am named. Joy, *alegría, feliz,* Feliciano.

(Across town, a woman wakes alone in the hospital, groggy, her breasts bound and leaking. The nurses won't tell her anything. No one visits her. She rises and packs, moving slowly around the sterile room.)

*   *   *

We visit Key West every year, driving from Miami when I'm a baby, flying from England on 747s, flying from West Virginia later on. We come when my cousins are there; the old house on Elizabeth Street is full of children.

Papi sits in his brown rocker facing the wall, listening to Spanish radio turned low, doing Spanish crosswords and search-a-words. He speaks no English, and we speak no Spanish. We avoid him; he's strange. There's plenty to do outside. We don't remember being held on his lap in the black-and-white photos.

Just before we leave, we're sent into the room where he sits. The rocker shifts slightly and turns out to face us. It's a ritual our parents put us through every time. In his forties when my father was born, Papi is ancient now, unreal. Everything about him is a blunted square, everything brown or gray: his chair, his chest in its shirt, his head.

"Remember Papi," he croaks. He pulls dollar bills from his breast pocket and gives one to each of us. Eager, guilty, trying not to appear greedy but relieved to earn something for our discomfort, we take them. We look in his watery eyes and say, "*Gracias,*" the sum of our Spanish.

"Remember Papi," he says again, looking at us, and a single tear tracks slowly down his cheek, like the Indian looking at the landfill in the commercial I've seen on TV. "Remember Papi."

Sometimes he clutches us to his chest, patting our backs with a bent hand. The gray bristles of his cheek scratch me. I can feel the wordless desperate love pouring all over me through his grasp, and despite myself, despite my eagerness to escape out into the bright sun with my cousins — despite the child's stiffening and pulling away that I try, from politeness, to control — I love him back.

Nanny can't abide my lazy ways. "Sweep," she says, handing me a broom and pointing to the long driveway rolled flat as a bedsheet from Elizabeth Street to the print shop. I stand in the sun, my hands gripped around the wood, pushing the thin silt side to side.

"I don't know how to sweep," I wail when she comes out to chide me. It's true. My mother grew up in Waukegan, in a world where the mothers clean and the children play: she leaves me to my devices. But Nanny quit school in seventh grade to help take care of her little brothers and sisters. Idle girls make her nervous.

"Crazy. Crazy like your father, but with the books. Always your nose in a book. *Mira,*" she says, handing me a sponge in the kitchen. "Wipe."

When her big sister died, she married the widower and kept his house and raised his child and gave him four more. She washed their clothes and gave them baths and woke at five to start cooking the hot lunches for the men who'd come in sweaty from the print shop at noon to sit at the long table in the kitchen. Black beans and saffron rice and garlic pork and applesauce, *papas rellenos* and tamales, and for dessert, fresh key lime pie and sliced mangoes from the yard.

My aunts could clean a house and cook a meal by the time they were ten, and even my father, Nanny's only son — and her favorite, my aunts said, for no good reason other than he was a damn boy — even he could clean a bathroom, wash dishes, fry an egg to change your life. My aunt Linda got so good at cleaning houses that when she grew up she did it for a living in Miami, and the people liked her work so much, fast and quiet and leaving no dust, they gave her things: toys that still worked, kitchen appliances, suits that were old but still very nice, good quality even if not so stylish.

Every summer we fly to Miami and drive down the linked bridges to stay, sleeping in rooms painted light green, pale lilac, my parents in one, the girl cousins allowed to sleep over with me in the other. Whispering, giggling, we fall asleep to the whir of electric fans propped in each window. The windows are screened, but red bumps rise on our legs in the morning. We count them, on our backs with our legs straight up, the sheets kicked aside in a tangle, and the one with the most is the sweetest.

Those rooms are kept darkened all day, their clattery green

blinds shut tight. We can't play there — even our Barbies have to come outside under the mango trees to play in the rot of damp leaves.

We run races down the driveway, screaming, our rubber sandals spanking the bright cement, our hands smacking the print shop wall in triumph. Outside, we never have to be quiet.

Inside, Nanny and the aunts hear everything and want us to shut up. So we sit on the cool tile of the front porch, taking turns two at a time on the swing. We walk down to the candy store, jumping over the great banyan roots that split the sidewalk, and spend all our money, or we beg a grown-up to take us fishing off the docks, the little bluegills and sunfish that my father cleans in seconds, swish, a silvery scatter of scales in the dust. At the beach, he climbs coconut palms and tosses the coconuts down to us. He cracks them on rocks and gives us the sweet watery milk.

Back at the house, we sit on the steps that run up the outside of the house to where the renters live. The seventh step is the highest we're allowed to go, so we sit on the eighth, right on the edge, poised to scoot down the second a grown-up comes out. We sit by the open window and listen, braiding each other's hair and practicing in low voices.

"Damn boys," I start, lulled by Susie's quick fingers against my neck.

"Damn," she says, sounding just like Nanny but with a voice rounder and smoother. "Damn it," she says, her teeth clenched around a barrette. "Damn those damn boys anyway."

The driveway's a swimming pool now. Two interior decorators from Miami bought it when Papi died and Nanny moved to the retirement apartments. I visited her there once on spring break, when I was seventeen. She kept showing me how easy everything was to take care of, how small the rooms were, how quick to vacuum. She and the old ladies sat around talking about how they wanted their funerals to be.

The print shop is a guest cabana.

When my father was a boy, he was crazy for the movies. He wanted to do it all — make, write, be in and around movies. Every Saturday he walked to the Strand or the San Carlos, sitting through two or three showings in a row. When he was twelve, he owned little reels you could buy at the camera store — Laurel and Hardy, Buster Keaton — and he would show them on the celadon wall of the print shop on Sundays, a nickel an hour to the neighborhood kids. He was going to be directing the movies one day, he told them, and starring in them, too, when he felt like it. But there wasn't money for film school, for college, for anything. He started out driving a truck instead, then the wheelchairs, and then he worked his way up to marketing and PR.

Four minutes of home movie still exist, filmed when he was seventeen, the year before he left home. My father sits me down in his living room, a thousand miles away. I'm thirty-two, visiting him in West Virginia. It's snowing.

"Okay, watch now," he says. The tape starts rolling. "*Mira, mira*," he says, tapping my arm when the focus clears. *Look*. The colors are bright with that strange garishness of old color films.

Uncle Mario is setting type, screwing the letters into the rectangular frame. He pulls a lever; it slaps into place. Papi slices what looks like a machete through reams of fresh paper.

In one scene, shot from a tripod, my father the teenager stacks neat dozens of notepads and wraps them in tan parcel paper. His hair is slicked down, black, shining. His khakis are belted. His eyes are young and brown.

No one looks at the camera, which makes it all seem very serious: a documentary of printing in the 1950s in Key West.

"I told them to do that," my father says eagerly. "I kept telling them not to look up at me." No one does.

*   *   *

Now, to stay in the bed-and-breakfast for a week costs a month's worth of my salary. Tony and I are planning to take our father and stepmother there, as a surprise, when he calls to say she's left him.

We had talked to her about the trip, not knowing their breakup was imminent, and she'd discouraged the idea; she didn't think he'd be interested. But we'd gone ahead and planned it anyway. We'd pay for everything; how could they object?

On the phone, at a loss for ways to console him, I tell him about our plan, adding impromptu modifications to downplay her absence: a week in the old house on Elizabeth Street during the Christmas holiday, all of us together, his children, his grandchild, in the house where he'd grown up. He can walk around the island and show Grey all the things he did as a boy. He is stunned.

"This makes me so happy, honey," he says, his voice thick. "You don't know how happy this makes me." He's silent for a ragged moment. "Nothing has made me this happy for a long time," he finally says, with tears in his voice. "That you two would do that. Would want to do that for me." He brightens, talking about the things we'll do; his voice sparks with the old verve. We talk about the places we'll have to see, the street vendors' *bollitos* Grey's never tasted.

But long before Christmas, he's dead.

6

Even in the black-and-white wedding photos, my mother's eyes have a touch of sleaze, a come-hither Joan Collins glint. My father's face is young, eager, shining; he looks toward her. She looks at the camera, chin lowered, one white satin toe pointed forward, eyes leveling their invitation.

Once, my mother and some other stewardesses partied on a yacht with O. J. Simpson, she tells me when I'm nine. I think how much fun it would be: throwing footballs on the deck, eating cake all day.

We are in Bridgeport, West Virginia, where we have moved to get away from the Miami girlfriend. Aunt Lou lives there; it's where she moved when she married a man from the naval base in Key West. They built a house next door to his family's cattle farm. My father was fired for charging lingerie and hotel getaways on the company credit card, my mother tells me, and that's why we left Miami.

Now he's the vice president of marketing and public relations for a little airline. These airplanes have propellers, and there's only one seat on each side of the aisle.

In Bridgeport, my father takes us for ice cream, Tony and me.

We stop to pick up a friendly lady. She has short brown hair and freckles and laughs a lot and says what nice children we are, and we like her, but we don't see her anymore.

My mother sits me down on the front porch to have a talk with me. I know what she is going to say. All the fourth grade girls have already been shepherded into Mrs. Clevenger's room at school to watch the filmstrip — grainy men in white lab coats and blobby pink cells moving under the microscope — while the boys play kick-ball outside.

My mother opens the youth book, the red one with chapters on drugs and dating, to the blank white pages at the back. She draws something that looks like a goat's head. The curling horns, it turns out, are my ovaries, and the goat's face is my womb. There will be blood and pain and messy pads that come loose, and you can get pregnant, so stay away from boys because it's like a chain: the first link is something simple, like holding hands, but all the links are connected, and once you start it's very hard to stop and sometimes you can't and then you're pregnant.

"Do you have any questions?" she asks. The yard looks green and cool. I'm eight years old.

"Is there any way of getting out of it?"

"Out of what?"

"All of it."

She laughs. This is a very funny remark. She repeats it to her women friends at the Kingdom Hall.

That year, we leave the small town of Bridgeport, moving to a farmhouse in the country, down a gravel road. It has thirteen rooms and two acres, centered in a valley — a holler, our neighbors say — full of farms with cows and horses, circled by mountains we're allowed to hike up. The front two rooms were the original log cabin: inside, you can run your hand along the silky wood. My father and uncle re-build the old porch, put on a new roof. To welcome us, our next-door neighbors bring over a bowl of barbecued groundhog.

We spend little time in the village, which is small: an old brick grade school, an old brick high school that's now the middle school, a Dairy Mart, a feed store. The Fourth of July parade goes down the main road and then turns around and comes back up again. Boys my age spit tobacco in the street.

Out on the land, our mother turns us loose — we can go where we want, hike anywhere we please. There are two ponds full of fish, trees to climb, and great strip-mined meadows cloaked in flowers on mountaintops. When my father and I climb them, we twirl like Julie Andrews, singing "The Hills Are Alive."

I've been promised a pony, and when I'm nine, my father buys an unbroken mare for twenty dollars from someone he works with at the airport. I curry her, stroke her nose, whisper in her hairy ears. Shaggy and resentful, she bucks me off and kicks. My arms are mauled black from her teeth. I adore her. She gallops hard and can jump the creeks that thread the valley. We climb the thin cow paths along the sides of hills. I ride her bareback through the high mead-ows, feeling wild and tough.

My brother, four, begins to have accidents. Left alone, he climbs the porch railing and falls ten feet to the rocks below, splitting his fore-head. It's an hour's drive to the hospital. He shows off the black whiskers of his stitches. His eyebrow grows back patchy.

He chases a guinea hen under the barn, and a protruding nail rips down his spine. More stitches. The silver scar runs down his back like the trail of a slug.

Tony's injuries terrify me. We've grown up knowing our mother will let us bleed to death for Jehovah. I stay closer to the house.

*   *   *

My mother has always loved things grown fresh. On road trips, she lugs us to pay-as-you-pick places, where we moan up and down the monotonous hot rows, filling our little peeled wood buckets, asking how much longer. She takes us for walks down dirt roads, where we scramble through ditches to pick the free blackberries.

"It's good for you," she insists. "One day you'll thank me."

When we move to the farmhouse, she rents a rototiller and plows up a ridiculously large portion of our land. She talks about Euell Gibbons, whose books she avidly reads, and about the Victory Garden her father had when she was a little girl. She plants corn, beans, peppers, squash, tomatoes, broccoli, lettuce. It's a full-scale operation. We're pressed into service, picking out rocks, weeding the endless rows. "I am going out of my mind with boredom," I yell across to Tony, loud, so she can hear. The soil is hard and light brown.

Each year, the neighbors' cows escape and wander in, destroying the crop, or deer eat the corn, or rabbits eat the lettuce, or there's a plague of June bugs, and our mother's lips clench in frustration at her dream, gone again. There's always enough of something left, though, to justify the boxes of Ball jars she buys in August, the kitchen filled with steam, her arms red and puffy as she pulls canned tomatoes or peppers out of the big metal pot with tongs. When they're cool, we help her carry them out to the cellar house, creepy with dark rotted smells and spiderwebs, where a potato bin big as a coffin lurks against the stone wall.

When the weather is icy, she sends us out to get jars of things she wants to make for dinner.

"I hate peppers," I say.

"Would you *please* just do what I ask, for once?" she says, her eyes suddenly flaring with damp exhaustion, and I feel guilty.

But we have no long-term sympathy. We want her to give it up.

It is the fifth grade, and the brick grade school will be my seventh school. Each year, we have moved. Each year, I have gone to a new classroom with a folded floral note from my mother, sealed with a gold foil circle, to give the teacher: I must not say the Pledge of Allegiance but must sit silently while the other children do. I must not partake of any birthday games or cupcakes. I must not make any Halloween, Christmas, or Easter decorations but must be excused from class to sit in the hallway while the other children do. If evolution is discussed in class, I must be excused to sit in the hall. The teacher would be welcome to call her at home if she has questions.

What the hallway is like. Green, echoey. The desk pulled against a wall. Other kids with hall passes staring as they walk by. The wide doorways into other halls. In Miami, flat orange carpeting. In West Virginia, the floors are cement painted gray, with black scuffmarks laced in patterns, thin in places, thick in places, like the strokes of a Chinese brush.

I fold my arms on the desk and put my face down on them. The dark crevices of my skin are ledges in a cave. Tiny people are building a fire, climbing up the ledges, or looking out the chinks to check for bears.

Fifth grade is a new chance, but I don't have much hope. Before the bus comes, my stomach starts to churn and clench. I tell my mother it hurts. "Stop your whining," she says.

Jeans are worldly. Instead I wear the polyester double-knit outfits my mother selects, blue pants with a sailboat sewn onto the ankle, a matching blue shirt with a sailboat appliquéd on the chest. Culottes. Clothes that are modest. It is hopeless. I am as marked as Cain.

Because I've been skipped ahead, I am two years younger than everyone else. I don't like the same things. I do stuff they say is dorky.

I may not go to a worldly party. I may not spend the night at a worldly girl's house. I may not play a sport. I may not join a club that meets after school. "Bad associations spoil useful habits," my mother quotes again and again. "First Corinthians 15:33." If another girl is friendly to me, I am to take the opportunity to witness to her. How many Witness books can I place at school? "Think of it as a challenge," my mother says.

Teachers excuse me from my regular class so I can go to gifted, where we do interesting stuff instead of worksheets: build a container so you can drop an egg off the third floor and it won't break. But the other kids stare when I leave. I come back later in the day, embarrassed, slipping into my chair, not meeting anyone's eyes. No one will tell me what the assignments were.

They threaten, but no one hits. They get me alone in the gym, the hall, the bathroom. They crowd around me, the popular girls, the cheerleaders, or the girls who wish they were popular, shoving. Turn the other cheek, is what I've been told. I've seen the elder whose thumb is just a stump; he lost it in prison, where he had to go when he wouldn't go to war. We are conscientious objectors. We do not fight, do not involve ourselves in the conflicts of this wicked system of things. Do not talk back. Do not hit back if they hit you. If possible, try to witness.

At home, I sit on the black leatherette stool and cry directly onto the counter. My forehead gets cold and hurts. Sometimes my mother sits on the stool next to mine. "Paul reminds us to be joyful when we are persecuted for Jehovah's name's sake," she says. Her hand rubs lightly up and down my back.

Sometimes she gets fed up. "Would you just ignore them already?" she says, her tone impatient, the grooves crawling from the pink of her lip into the powdery tan makeup above it. "Quit whining about it." The boys slam me in the face with dodgeballs when Miss Noble goes to get a drink.

Adam and Eve were created by God six thousand years ago. I hum Kingdom Hall songs in my head when the teacher talks about prehistoric civilizations and continental migration. All history is pointless to learn. This system of things is temporary; it will vanish in the twinkling of an eye. God's Kingdom is coming. College would be pointless, my mother tells me when I ask about it. Good Witnesses don't need college, unless they're going to be doctors or nurses for other Witnesses. Armageddon will happen before I'm grown up, and if it doesn't, I will marry a nice brother, have children, and be a housewife, like my mother. So what would be the point of college? The end is near.

Without thinking about it, I get straight A's. While the teacher talks, I draw pictures in the margins of my notebooks: Hank, the girl I really am, a cowgirl with blond braids and chaps. I give her the bell-bottomed jeans I wish I had and invent stories for her until the bell rings.

All sums of money I calculate in units of horse models, the realistic kind I like, Breyer, which cost seven dollars apiece. At dinner, my father mentions some figure in connection with the airline. "That's six hundred and fifty horse models," I say.

All my allowance from chores is funneled toward their purchase. I worship their dark eyes, sleek bodies. I build matching families of them — mare, stallion, foal — and carry them down to the creek, where they stomp and snort in the sand, fording rough waters to save each other.

In the winter, my green-and-brown carpet serves as their grass.

"Can't you pick those things up? You could put them right there, on top of your dresser," my mother says, irritable. "Neatly." A dozen of them are scattered around my floor in small groupings.

"They need room to graze," I say, not looking up.

My double bed is a covered wagon, and Tony and I are headed out to the frontier. We sit on pillows by the footboard. I chatter rapidly, trying to get him to stay, describing everything to him, telling him things I've read in the Little House books and things I make up. He's five now, restless, difficult to lure. Antsy, my mother says. Pa and Ma are sleeping in the back with Carrie, and the two of us get to drive. For hours while it snows outside our windows, we sit or scoot around on the bed, or jump down to talk with a friendly Swede about what lies up ahead. Pet and Patty trot before us, and Jack follows behind, tail wagging.

We pray chronically. At the beginning and end of every meeting, three times a week, the brother prays for us and we say *Amen.*

Before every meal at home, our mother prays, until we're old enough to ask the blessing.

> Dear Father in heaven, Jehovah, we come before you tonight to ask your blessing on this food we are about to eat, and to thank you for your many wonderful gifts. We ask you to keep us mindful of your purpose, oh Jehovah, and lead us not into temptation, and forgive us when we fall short. Keep our eyes on the prize of the Paradise earth you have promised to us, and help our brothers and sisters around the world who are undergoing persecution for spreading the good news of your kingdom. Help them to be strong and persevere. Help us, too, to remain steadfast in your name. All these things we ask of you, in the name of your son, Jesus Christ, Amen.

I pray silently each night in bed. I pray for my brother and my pony, that they are kept safe from harm, and that I might be given more horse models.

I read *Black Beauty,* the Black Stallion series by Walter Farley, and all the horse books by Marguerite Henry: *Misty of Chincoteague, Sea Star, Black Gold.* I read anthologies of stories about girls and their horses.

My fifth grade teacher, Mrs. Dolan, is tall and beautiful with dark hair that flips up on the ends like Jackie Kennedy's. She has a soft voice and is always kind. One day, she puts her arm around me after class and gives me a horse poster, because all my writing assignments are about horses. She has soft dark eyes like Bambi's mother.

I am not like the other girls I know. My cousin Jeri, who is worldly, has posters of Shaun Cassidy and Parker Stevenson, smiling against a blank blue background. One of my Kingdom Hall friends has Leif Garrett, Peter Frampton. Her mother lets her, even though they're worldly.

My walls are covered with horse posters and pictures, my own drawings of horses and the paint-by-numbers of horses' heads I have laboriously and impatiently painted, disappointed with my results, which do not look like the pictures on the boxes they came in.

In college, I read *Equus*: horses, violence, Jesus, sex — all blended in a sweet and toxic cocktail, intimately familiar. I memorize Dr. Dysart's final speech as my monologue for auditions.

This is before I make myself stop acting, when I realize that it has become far too easy to become someone else, to slip into someone fictional's mind and gestures and way of being, and too slow a wrench, more difficult each time, to reinhabit myself.

In sixth grade, I am made a patrol. I strap on the orange plastic belt and carry the yellow flag, even in snow. Sometimes it's fun — with the other patrol kid, our flags moving in unison, like a pageant — keeping the little kids safe while they cross. In the stairways inside the building, we watch to make sure no one is taking two steps at a time, which would be unsafe. "One step at a time," we yell. "No gum!"

One crossing is down the hill, down a long flight of cement steps, which can't be seen from the school. The head cheerleader and I are assigned to work it. She hates me: I am her special target. For four years, she threatens to beat me up or kill me. She tells me to take the far side, and I take it. After all the kids have crossed, two friends of hers appear: Marvin and Teresa, cousins, tall, thick-bodied kids with different shades of blond hair. There's no snow yet, but the air is cold. They circle me, Marvin throwing punches that don't connect.

"You smart-ass bitch," the cheerleader says, shoving her flag-pole at me with both hands. "Think you're so smart." No cars come down the road. "Straight-A bitch. What are you going to do now?"

"Yeah, what are you going to do?" Teresa says, hands on hips.

I don't meet their eyes. "I guess I'm going to go put this flag away."

"Fat chance you are," says the cheerleader. "You're going to get pulverized, is what's going to happen."

"Why don't you fight back? Why don't you fight back, you big baby?"

My eyes are hot, my hands clenched around the wooden flag-pole. "Because I'm not supposed to."

"Not supposed to. Not supposed to. Is it *against your religion,* you big fucking whiny baby?" It's a phrase they hear a lot.

I can feel the beginnings of tears, so I think fast. "What do you want me to do?" I say quickly. "Let's just get it over with. Do you want to beat me up? Come on. Beat me up."

They shift on their feet. Marvin and Teresa eye the cheerleader, watching for her signal.

"Do you want to hear me say I'm afraid?" I say loudly. "Because it's true that I am afraid. I am. Who wouldn't be?" *Three to one?* I think but don't say. "I'm afraid." I yell it. "I'm afraid!"

They laugh uneasily. "Forget this," the cheerleader says, lowering her pole, and they mutter, their voices disgusted, as they climb the long narrow flight of steps up the hill toward school, their backs to me.

I stand on the sidewalk. It's winter, and the light is already growing dusky at three-thirty. My hands shake. Finally, a pickup passes, and then I cross back over.

Riding home on the bus each afternoon, I think about which buildings I'm going to live in after Armageddon, when Jehovah destroys all the worldly people and only Witnesses are left.

I'll live most of the time in the Sheraton Hotel in Harrisburg, where our father has taken us. It has a big swimming pool with fake rocks, a waterfall, and a slide, and real palm trees growing, all of it inside a huge glass-roofed atrium that's warm in the winter. My horses and lions will live there with me. There's a cocktail bar made like an old mill with a water wheel that turns.

All the worldly people will disappear in the twinkling of an eye. Good-bye, Missy Settrick. Good-bye, Jeff Hyde. I'll be swimming.

At ten, my loves are numerous, excessive: the field behind our house, my pony, my brother. I write extravagant love letters to my father when he travels on business.

Melodramatic, my mother calls me. I nauseate her, she says. I sicken her with my ridiculous displays. I am absurd.

I withdraw. In her presence, I wear a polite and careful mask. Out of her sight, I carry my brother everywhere in my arms. I curry the pony at sunset, singing.

Indiscriminately, I read: the Bobbsey Twins, Nancy Drew, unabridged copies of *The Three Musketeers* and *Ivanhoe.* The Bobbsey Twins books are my favorites, lilac-spined mystery after mystery lined up in numbered order in my bedroom cupboard.

The older set of twins, Nan and Bert, with dark hair and eyes, solve the mysteries and protect the younger twins, the golden-curled Freddie and Flossie. All the children are unerringly good, kind, responsible, giving their toys to the poor. They notice details, track down clues, bravely ask strange grown-ups questions to bring the bad guys to justice.

One afternoon, when I am ten and my mother and brother are gone somewhere, my father brings a woman to the house. She is young, pretty, with wide blue eyes. She will be painting his portrait, he tells me, in costume. She pushes her long blond hair back over her shoulders and sets up an easel.

I know who she is; I've seen her at rehearsals. At night, I run lines with my father. I've learned all the songs by heart, and when my mother lets me, I go with him to the Clarksburg community theater to watch. Onstage, the woman wears a blue bikini top, filmy pants, and a green plastic jewel glued into her navel. Her part is not a speaking part. She just sways around with some other girls.

She's twenty-one, she says when I ask her. In the living room, she squeezes colors onto a palette, and my father arranges himself in a chair, wearing his maroon costume with a wreath of fake leaves on his head. It's ancient Rome. His character is Senex, the old man who betrays his wife for a young girl who doesn't want him.

She begins to paint. They laugh and joke together. Her laugh is a sweet sound, and her movements as she paints are gentle. I sit on the leather couch, watching.

"Would you like a glass of water?" I ask.

"Well, yes," she says. "That would be very nice." To my father, she murmurs, "She's so polite."

"Do you like horses?" I say.

She looks at me, and her tone is surprised. "Why, yes. I love horses. I used to ride," she says.

"I'll get you my favorite glass, then. It has a zebra on it." I leave the room and find it in the kitchen cupboard, one of a set of glasses with animals — a tiger, a giraffe, an elephant — staring out through high green grass. I turn on the tap and let the water run cold, tapping my finger into the stream the way my mother does. I fill the glass. And then a funny thing happens.

The house is quiet. I can hear them laughing in the other room. My father sings a bar: "You're lovely, absolutely lovely," and I have the sudden certainty that my mother doesn't know she's here. I stand in my mother's kitchen, listening to them laugh, and I lean over the glass, looking outward through the cool water.

I'm the one who runs lines with my father. I'm the one who feeds him his cues each evening, the one who has learned all his songs. From inside the glass, seen through the water, the grass blades wave, and the zebra's face contorts in the clear afternoon light.

I let drop a mouthful of spit. It floats in a bubbly blob on the top. I shake the glass until it swirls down, invisible. Then I walk back.

"Here," I say. I smile like giving people water is my favorite thing to do.

"Thank you." She takes it.

We all smile at each other

When my mother comes to get me, I'm reading in my room. I know that the book, *Logan's Run,* is too sexy, that I am reading on borrowed time: if my mother looks closely at it, she will take it away, so I'm reading as quickly as I can. So far, she thinks of it as something like *Star Wars* or *Battlestar Galactica,* which she lets us watch and which we imitate, hauling around the big yellow canister vacuum cleaner and its many hoses, our weapons, shooting at aliens from behind chairs.

Our parents have called us into the family room, where the TV and the furnace are, the warmest room in the old house, which they've been dismayed to discover has drafts everywhere. There's a gold rug and our old familiar couch from before I was born, reupholstered in orange-and-brown plaid. We sit. Our parents face us.

They will be separating, they say. Our father will be moving into an apartment in a town about half an hour away, but he will see us every week, and we can visit him. They have been having problems, they say, grown-up problems. This is for the best. Our mother smiles, clasping her hands together so the knuckles poke out pale. Their plan is to take six months to reflect on their relationship, and then he will probably come back home. They still love each other, they say, and they both love us very much, and this is not in any way our fault. They both look anxious, searching our faces.

"Do you have any questions?" they say. There is a long silence. The room feels very warm, and they look small and far away.

"Can I go finish my book?" I ask.

*   *   *

But he does not come back home. Before six months are even over, people have seen him with the new girlfriend, the blond twenty-one-year-old who came to paint his portrait.

"That was not the deal," our mother says over and over in the empty kitchen, crying, slamming cupboards. She files for divorce. "That was just not the deal."

She drinks a pot of coffee every morning and begins to lose weight. When friends comment, she says, "Yeah, I just lost a hundred and sixty pounds of ugly fat. I got a divorce." She says it in a tough voice.

At night, she cries. "I thought it wouldn't last. That he'd get it out of his system. I thought she was just like the others."

But she is not like the others. Two years later, he marries her, and twenty-four years later — when he's retiring, when she's leaving him — he puts a bullet in his head.

7

After the divorce, my mother's first entrepreneurial effort fails. She opens a resale clothing shop and gives it a clever name: *Encore*. But in small-town West Virginia, people's used finery is a shabby thing. Her clientele has none of the chic-girl-down-on-her-luck wit the name deserves. Instead of Jean Rhys heroines, she attracts fat, bad-smelling women who slap their kids. There is nothing vintage to find. Her racks hold only the same clothes that once hung at Hill's and Heck's, the budget department stores. But dingier, with the smell of stale closets. At the counter, irritated women claim their things are worth more than she thinks.

All my father's record albums are gone, and my mother buys a new one of her own, with white blobs of ink in the shape of Barry Manilow performing on a dark blue background. "I want to be somebody's baby, I don't want a child of my own," my mother belts out, dusting swiftly with a rag and Pledge. "I was the one who was always strong, and I was always the one left alone."

I follow her into the next room, and she doesn't say, *Would you get out from underfoot?* as she usually does.

She just works around me, fast and vigorous. "I was the one understanding, and letting the other go free," she sings loudly, her voice hard and happy. "Now I want to be somebody's baby, let somebody worry 'bout me."

She plays it over and over again, singing, until the whole downstairs smells like lemons.

The two years after my parents divorce are a lonely time. Tony and I ride the bus home together, unlock an empty house.

I make our after-school snacks in white Corelle bowls: a heap of Golden Grahams on the bottom, then instant chocolate pudding I make in the blender, then chocolate ice cream, then Hershey's syrup, with powdered vanilla malt, our father's favorite from the jar he left behind, on top. We sit with our mountains of goo, sucking our spoons, watching our programs, and wait for our mother to call.

Sometimes she's home in time to fix dinner; other evenings, she tells me what to defrost and put in the oven. I do my schoolwork at the kitchen counter and make sure Tony finishes his. I watch to make sure he doesn't get into anything. Sometimes, when I hate him, when I want to be anywhere but watching a little boy for hours, I taunt him. I use my mother's tone and say the things she says until we both cry. He hits, wordless with frustration, his fists shooting out. Once he chases me through the house with a knife. Mostly we are companionable, two kids saddled with each other in a lonely house for hours.

I hate to shop for clothes with my mother. I'm drawn to whatever looks beautiful, but she always goes straight to the big red *SALE* signs. "Where do you think you're going?" she barks out across the racks. "Get over here," she says sharply, loudly. "You think we can afford that kind of thing?" I learn to stay next to her rather than risk embarrassment.

But I discover that embarrassment works both ways. Sometimes, when we go into a fancy department store for the perfume or makeup she wears, I pretend I am retarded. I walk with a limp and let my head fall to the side, knocking my bent hand against my chest, the fingers flopping loosely. In those moments, I am the opposite of what she expects me to be — smart, polite, tidy, invisible. I let my mouth hang open.

"Stop that," she hisses. I keep doing it. "You stop that. We are *in public,* young lady." But I know she won't hit me in the luxury stores, where people are genteel and she's always anxiously brittle.

I utter a guttural moan.

"Fine," she says, turning away, "enjoy yourself." She walks swiftly up the aisle.

"Mommy," I cry in a sloppy, loud, retarded voice, staggering after her. "Don't leave me!" Women turn to watch. "Don't leave me, Mommy!" I wail.

She hurries back, grabs my hand, and jerks me along beside her. The elegant women with smooth hair turn back to their browsing, heads shaking, eyebrows raised. "You are really going to get it, young lady," she whispers harshly. Later, I do.

They expose us to strange juxtapositions, my parents. My mother, brother, and I drive from our grandmother's house in Waukegan, where we're visiting, to Milwaukee, where an assembly is being held in a stadium. It's hot. The days go on forever. Truth and more truth.

At the beginning of one of the sessions — when we're all still getting settled in our seats, fanning ourselves with the programs, shuffling book bags and cups of cold soda — the brother far, far below on the constructed platform asks if anyone's had the chance to see *Saturday Night Fever,* which is still in theaters there in the city. Hands go up around us and speckle the distance, but my mother sits primly, as if she knows what's coming.

"Then brothers and sisters," he thunders, "you should be ashamed of yourselves." It is an obscene movie, he tells us, not fit for the children of Jehovah. How can we be pure if we pollute our minds with such filth, with images of fornication and ungodly behavior? How can we preach the good news of God's Kingdom to the worldly when our eye is not single and full of light? He goes on and on. Our mother, who will not watch R-rated films, is radiating that holy look, her chin held high.

I have not seen it, but I feel vaguely guilty because I know all the words to the soundtrack.

Not long before, our father had devoted a long weekend to taking us to the Kentucky Horse Park for the inaugural International Equestrian Olympics. We saw steeplechases, Lipizzan stallions, glossy draft horses pulling impossible loads. I was in horse-girl heaven. My brother, five, was less thrilled but interested in all the dirt and how things worked. Our father waited patiently for us to have seen enough.

All the hours there and back in his long blue secondhand Oldsmobile, he played his new eight-track of the Bee Gees, and we sang. On the way home, I lay down across the dark backseat, falling asleep to the rapid cool pulse of their falsetto.

I have my mother to myself for four days. We're driving the furniture store truck to North Carolina, choosing furniture from a dealer's show, and driving back to Bridgeport with her purchases. She's the cofounder, co-owner of the store. It does not occur to me, at eleven, to realize that she is brave.

Each time we stop, she buys Pepsis and Peppermint Patties or Three Musketeers bars for us both. There's no stereo, so we talk. I ask questions. Jehovah's rules on premarital sex seem a little pointless to me, given the development of birth control. The Old Testament had its purposes, but it got written a long time ago. If sex no longer results in unwanted babies, what's Jehovah's problem with it?

My mother doesn't like this line. Her upper lip wrinkles stiffly. I persist.

"Well, did you ever have sex with Dad before you got married? Or"— and I am dizzy at the vastness of the thought —"with someone else before you met Dad?"

She glances sharply at me and turns her eyes back to the road. "That, young lady," she snaps, "is none of your business."

I snort Pepsi through my nose, helpless.

"What's so funny?"

"I'm not stupid."

"What's that supposed to mean?"

"I'm a kid, Mom; I'm not dumb." The more I laugh, the tighter her mouth gets. "If you say it's none of my business, then you did."

Her hands bulge bony on the wheel and her mouth clamps down in the pucker that means she won't be noticing my existence for at least an hour, that again I've crossed that fatal, shifting line. But it's worth it. And her eyes, as I watch her, seem to wear the sheen of amusement.

In the Kingdom Hall, I sit with my ankles crossed under the chair, a metal, stackable chair with tweedy orange cushions for seat and back. The metal tube with its squared edges sprouts above the back cushion and curves down again, a kind of handle, for when the brothers gather and stack the rows of chairs. I want to lean forward and touch it, grab it, rock the chair in front, but I don't. The brother at the microphone is reading aloud the paragraphs I read to myself yesterday. All my answers are underlined in my book.

I rub my legs against each other, very slightly, back and forth. In one direction, the feeling is rough, like all the threads of the panty hose are quarreling. In the other, it's smooth. I let my eyes fall half closed and imagine I'm in a forest with Ricky Gibson, two rows ahead. I'm in front on the path, riding my dappled white horse and clad in a flowered dress like the girl in the Jontue commercial, and he follows, besotted, on foot, up the narrow trail, knowing the clearing we are making for, the clearing where we will have lots of sex, which consists of kissing and rolling on the ground together with my dress riding up my legs, my hair blowing across my wild enchanting eyes the way the girl's does on television.

We stand to sing. I swivel around a little, until I can see Steve Starky sitting with his sisters and parents several rows behind. When we sit back down for the next talk, I imagine the whole thing again, but with him.

When the meeting is over, everyone heads toward the foyer of the Hall, with its rough shining tile and the rock waterfall as high as my shoulders, with a pool at the bottom. The little kids gather there, watching the goldfish, orange, pale gold, and white ones with red spots. They do not drop pennies because that would be wishing for good luck. To believe in luck is to invite Satan, like playing with a Ouija board or one of those black balls that answer questions. You can open your fortune cookie in a Chinese restaurant, but you cannot take the fortune seriously.

The older kids stand around by the long coatracks, boys talking to boys, girls talking to girls, everyone glancing across at each other.

Adults are clotted everywhere, talking in groups of three or four, lined up at the book counter where the brother stocks them up on things they need, things they might place at householders' doors that afternoon.

The mural behind the platform shows Paradise earth, after Armageddon has cleansed away the wicked. Lions and wolves lie in the grass with lambs, and a happy white family — mother, father, two children — opens a picnic lunch. Everything is beautiful, peaceful. Light glows on their joyful faces, on the snowcapped mountains.

My mother wears thin-heeled d'Orsay pumps that make her hips jut side to side as she walks up the aisle of the Kingdom Hall. She is glamorous, though I don't know it. I learn it later, as an adult, looking at old photographs. There it is: she is slender, elegant in capri pants, sunglasses, and sandals with straps thin as a bracelet. Headbands and scarves pull back her hair, which is here blond, here red-gold, here the blue-black I remember, fluffed in little curls cropped short near her face.

At eleven, I am taller than my mother. She gives me her yellowed wedding gown for dressing up; it's nothing she cares about now. But already I don't fit in it. Its shoulders don't span mine. My feet are larger than hers. Size eight, then nine, then ten. She squeezes my unsatisfactory hands, strange oblongs: "Marshmallow hands," she calls them, stretching out her own manicured fingers, slim in their rings, to compare. I bite my nails. I'm a head taller than my girl cousins, born the year I was. What kind of woman can I possibly become? What sort of woman made me?

I write a story about a girl who saves a barn full of horses from a fire. *Thundering hooves beat a drumming tattoo on the chilly autumn morn,* it opens, heavy with adjectives. My mother types it for me and tells me she is proud.

She used to write stories herself, she says, when she was a stewardess, before she knew my father. I am fascinated to hear about this; she never talks about the time before my father, except to say she ran away when she was eighteen — but eighteen seems grown-up to me, a normal, uninteresting age at which to move away from home, so I never pursue it. Her dream was to be a nurse, she tells me once, pressing a Cherry Ames book on me — she had read and loved the series as a girl — but her family had no money for nursing school. So she took what she had — her beauty, her ambition, her quickness to learn — and became a stewardess.

She takes the stories down from a cupboard, out of a box, sheaves of typing paper brown at the edges, a coffee-colored shadow seeping toward the blocks of print. I read them. They're about stewardesses.

In one, a stewardess exclaims to another, "You know, I do believe your eyes change color, depending on what you're wearing!"

"I know," the other woman replies lightly. "I'm waiting for them to turn orange, so I can wear a new dress I bought."

I think this is the height of wit. And I am fascinated: my mother's eyes change color — gray, green, blue, hazel. So this happened to her, once, and she said that clever thing, or wished later that she had.

Across the frontispiece of my green Bible spreads a map called "The Ancient World Before Our Common Era." It extends down to Ethiopia and over to Persia. *Mediterranean* is in parentheses, underneath the large capitals *THE GREAT SEA*. When I am bored during a talk, I lower my eyes toward it. Seventeen little men in costumes dot the map, each in the garb of his region: Sheba, Chaldea, Media, Egypt, Libya, Sicily, Crete. My favorite is the svelte man in the land of the Hittites, who looks like a flapper, his hair in bangs. I wish they had women in costume. There's one that might be a woman, way over in Tarshish, the only place where two people stand next to one another like a couple. The shorter figure has a pointy cap and things over his ears like Princess Leia.

Cities are marked — Babylon, Sidon, Tyre, Jerusalem, Jappa, Nineveh, Ur — and rivers. Near the black splotches of the Ararat mountains, a caption next to a tiny *x* reads *Garden of Eden?*

In Arabia, three camels plod through dunes. In Egypt, three pyramids mark Cairo, where I swam in the Sheraton pool in inflatable orange armbands and a Frenchman called me a *leetle feesh*. A whale splashes in the Mediterranean, and a sailing boat pulses with a dozen oars.

But the most fascinating character is in northern Africa, a land unmarked by cities or people. There, a nondescript dinosaur wanders, a contemporary of the Israelites, its body upright with little front paws like a tyrannosaurus, its head smooth and curving like pictures of a diplodocus or brontosaurus. Africa, with no people at all.

*   *   *

Andrea, Kay, and Sabine move to town from Detroit and join our congregation. They are young, single, and black: full-time pioneers. Not only are they supremely good in the eyes of Jehovah, they are, to me, supremely glamorous. Twenty-one, twenty-two: the age of freedom and power. They wear big gold hoop earrings.

Andrea and Kay stay briefly at our farmhouse — we have plenty of space. In the mornings, their metal combs lie licked by blue on the gas range. They let me watch in the bathroom as they singe their hair straight.

My mother invites them to drive to Florida with us in a borrowed RV. We stop to hike down to the lookout at New River Gorge and take a picture: Andrea, Kay, my brother, and me against the railing, his hood drawn around his little face against the cold. Our mother is strangely, singularly happy, snapping the photo, composing an image of a kind of family.

As we get farther south, the RV grows sultry, and Rod Stewart comes on the radio at night. His scratchy-voiced sex dirges sound different from the songbook litany I'm used to: obedience, modesty, humility, truthfulness. We must be chaste. We must never lie. His rough voice in the dark sounds dangerous and hungry, groping out raw toward the edges of things. "Oh, leave it on," Andrea says to my mother, and I pray silent thank-yous to Jehovah.

Each night in the bunk above the driver's seat, Kay rocks herself to sleep, propelling her body from side to side. She's asked us in advance not to laugh; she's always done it, doesn't know why. Each night the RV rocks for a while and then falls still.

In Miami, we stay with different brothers and sisters we knew when we lived there. We visit my mother's mother in Long Key, where she goes for the winters, and Nanny in Key West. Everywhere we stop, we go to the meetings. Everywhere, the format and schedule are the same, so we don't miss a thing.

* * *

My mother's business partner is another sister from the Kingdom Hall, a married woman with a son, seventeen. Her husband isn't a Witness.

My mother says disapprovingly that they eat out three meals a day, a waste of money. But I am fascinated. I want to live like that, from restaurant to restaurant, no cooking, no dishes — just talking and the food coming automatically.

The furniture store flourishes, and during the summer vacation I spend my days at the Bridgeport pool, the Benedum Library, or tucked with a book in a corner of the storage room, while my mother works. Sometimes, the other woman's son comes with his friend. They're Witnesses, so I can talk to them. I like them; Tom brings stacks of his old *Mad* magazines for me to read, and they tell jokes that break up the boredom of the long days. They tease me, pick me up and swing me around to say hello.

One day after they've driven off, my mother pulls me into her office, irritated, and shuts the door.

"Would you stop flirting with those boys?" she says. "It's disgusting, the way you throw yourself at them like that."

She starts going on dates with one of the single brothers whose houses she cleans. He is a pilot, a decade younger than she. At night, he takes her up in a Cessna.

Some nights she works late at the furniture store, nine or ten o'clock, and then goes out with him.

Tony and I are alone in the farmhouse, remote, surrounded by fields and cattle farms on a gravel road miles from the one-street town. The green wall phone rings in the kitchen.

"I want to play with your little pussy," says a man's voice, low and rough.

I drop the phone back on its metal cradle. All around, darkness shoves at the house. I check the locks, bring our dog Buddy and my brother into the family room with the TV, turn it up loud, shut the door.

When my mother gets home, she says, "Oh, just hang up on idiots like that."

Some nights, it is after eleven when she calls. The pilot wants to take her up to see the stars, just the two of them. She'll be just a little later.

"Please come home," I say, scared of the darkness, the phone calls, the fact that the caller knows I'm little. Is it someone on our road? Can he drive by and see that the Volkswagen's gone, that the lights are on in the house? Can he see us moving past the windows?

"Quit your whining," she says over the phone. "Do you have to ruin everything that's fun for me?"

"Please. Just come home."

"I'll be there when I get there."

One day while I'm at the library, she leaves my brother in the car and goes inside the pilot's house. The car is parked on a hill. She stays inside a long time. Tony climbs into the driver's seat to play race car.

They come out when they hear the crash. Two cars are damaged, and a third is totaled. Tony is uninjured, but he starts to wake up screaming from bad dreams.

He is a curious child. He likes to know how things work. He chains a cement block to the rear bumper of her Volkswagen to see what will happen. She beats him with a wooden spoon. He puts the garden hose into the exhaust pipe and turns on the water to see what will happen. She beats him again. While she's driving, he ties his shoelaces from the passenger-side door handle to the steering wheel and waits for her to turn left. She's talking to a sister in the backseat the whole time, doesn't notice what he's done until she's stuck in the middle of an intersection, horns blaring. She beats him, beats him, beats him. After a meeting late one Thursday night, he kicks in the spotlight that shines on the sign, "Kingdom Hall of Jehovah's Witnesses." It's starting not to seem like curiosity. She beats him in front of everyone, so that they can see she doesn't spare the rod.

She complains to her friends about how rambunctious he is, how difficult to control, how much she has to put up with. She believes it comes from red food coloring in his food, so we can't have hot dogs or Kool-Aid anymore.

In the mornings, she gives him big plastic cups full of cooled coffee from her pot, creamy with milk and sugar. She's done it from when he was little, from when he couldn't even say the word.

"Foffee?" he would beg, holding up the cup.

"Isn't that cute?" she'd say.

I've raised my son as himself, yes, but as a kind of pledge, too, to my brother, and to the world at large. Tall, confident, funny, Grey has never been struck or scorned. Held, loved, fed, picked up when he cried, listened to, praised. His education planned and saved for with care. Dozens of child psychology books, nutrition books, carefully read, starting from scratch, afraid of the template I'd inherited. All of it, some helpless attempt to redress what was my little brother's life, to say, *Sweetheart, this is what you deserved.*

In the rented van we drive to West Virginia for my father's funeral, I try to make it not so awful for my son. I think of the funerals I've seen in movies: times *when people come together* (the heavy, portentous tones of the voice-over guy), when they tell old family stories and laugh even though they're sad. So I tell Grey about the ingenious things my brother did as a kid: the shoelaces, the toaster he took apart. I tell the stories as though he's a mischievous imp, the way my mother told them at home, the way she bragged to Witness friends about what she had to put up with. My brother's mischief was part of our family lore. I leave out the beatings, which hang in the air-conditioned air around us.

"But how could your mom not notice the shoelace thing?" Grey asks my brother. He knows I couldn't have ignored him for that long when he was little.

"Yeah, go figure," my brother says. "I don't know." He's in the back bench seat with Cool Julie. "That's the million-dollar question."

Something occurs to me for the first time. "You know, how come you always came up with the crazy ideas when I wasn't around?" I ask. "I always had to hear about it later, when I got home from school or wherever."

"Are you kidding?" Tony says, and something in his tone makes me turn around to face him where he sits. "It didn't happen *because* you were there."

"What do you mean?"

"You wouldn't let it happen. You were always watching out for me." Cool Julie is nodding, like it's something they've discussed. "If I wanted to know what would happen if I did something, you would just tell me. You wouldn't let me pull that crazy crap."

Something closes up in my throat. I look at him.

"If you hadn't been there as much as you were," he says calmly, "I'd probably be dead."

Julie nods again. She's good for him, a no-bullshit kind of girl who lives out loud. I trust her.

"Yeah," she says. "Completely."

For years, I have felt guilty for failing my brother, failing to protect him, first from our mother's beatings and then from our stepfather's. Guilty, later, for not being able to help him financially, keep him in college, take care of him more.

I have never heard this, never put it together, never known I did something he values. I turn toward the front again and absorb it while the miles go by.

When we visit my grandmother in Waukegan, I find a box of Harlequin romances in her basement. My mother would take them away if she knew, so I read dozens down there in the cool damp dimness. In all of them, beautiful women in desperate circumstances appeal for help to arrogant, handsome men with lots of money. The men say harsh things and the women hate them but are beholden. Over time, they come to see all the good works the men have done secretly with their vast wealth — they've been tender to someone, a dog or an orphan — and the women happen to see. They begin to love the men — but oh, he does not even glance her way. What did that fiery kiss in the corridor mean, when he grabbed me and pressed his burning mouth to mine, his eyes dark and impenetrable? and then strode so brusquely away? But in the end, lo, they learn he's loved them all along.

The Kingdom Hall books explain nothing of this, preaching only the avoidance of sex and the happiness of duty in marriage. Even in marriage, masturbation is prohibited, and things I don't understand: oral sex, anal sex, adult mysteries the brothers mention on the platform and I don't ask about.

I stand alone in the dark basement hallway, kissing the back of my hand. At the Waukegan Kingdom Hall, I stare at the cutest boy who's close. When he glances up, I look down at my Bible.

My father has promised to build my pony a little barn, and to fence a section of our two acres. But he doesn't. He moves out.

In the summers, I stake her in the grass, her halter tied to a length of plastic twine. She grazes in wide loops.

We pay the neighbors to let her winter with their stock each year. She eats their hay, shelters in their barn, huddles with their horses until her thick pale coat starts to fall away and darken in the spring.

"One more expense," my mother says.

And then, the winter my father moves with his girlfriend into a garage apartment, my pony falls down the hill into the icy creek. When our neighbor goes out to feed, he finds her frozen body, her legs broken.

*   *   *

One summer day after she's finished at work, our mother drives us to
see the new house we might move into. We will have to sell the farmhouse, she says, eventually, and how much better to be in Bridgeport,
where the Kingdom Hall is, where her furniture store is.

Tony and I don't want to move. We've been in the farmhouse,
surrounded by acres of hilly pastureland, for three years. School is
awful, but it's familiar; there are kids who are newer than we are.
What will we do with Buddy, who runs free, chasing the chickens?

She turns the car toward Bridgeport Hill, the fanciest part of
town. I remember it from when I had gone to Johnson Elementary
School for fourth grade, when we'd first moved to West Virginia. If
you asked a girl where she lived, and she replied, "Bridgeport Hill,"
she would say it offhandedly, with a little toss of her head. We had
driven through it then, admiring the split-level houses and wide drive-
ways. But it had been too expensive, and not part of our mother's
dream of a rural Eden.

We wind down a quiet street and pull to a stop next to the curb,
idling in front of a two-story house with dark timbers and white
plaster, like old houses in Germany, with flowers tumbling from
boxes and spilling across the lawn. It's imitation, I can tell: everything is too new, and the slant of the roof is wrong. Still, it's pretty.
Evening sunlight pours across the grass, which is damp and green
and evenly cut. The garage has room for two cars, and new bicycles
lean in the driveway. Warm lights glow inside. Tony and I look at
each other, excited.

"Really?" I say.

Her answering laugh is harsh.

"No, not *really*." Her hands smack the steering wheel, and the
laugh keeps coming, a flat sound. "What's the matter with you? Do
you think we could afford a place like this on what your father pays?"
We deflate against our seats. "You'd better adjust your expectations,
let me tell you. I don't know what you kids are thinking."

She drives to another part of town, close to the furniture store, and stops in front of a bungalow with a small yard. There's trash in the grass, but we could pick it up.

"Now this," she says, "is more realistic. More along the lines of what I'm talking about." She snorts. "I don't know what kind of people you think we are."

I find and read my mother's paperbacks. She keeps them hidden. In one, rats assault a modern city, and everyone's dying of the plague. A politician's daughter sits on his lap, French-kisses him. He fondles her. They fuck with her on his lap saying *Daddy*. The protagonist's good girlfriend is knocked to the ground behind a Burger King and raped by a motorcycle gang, her orange-and-yellow uniform shoved up around her waist. She dies there, by the Dumpster. The protagonist, it is clear by the final page, is going to die. Everyone will die.

In another novel, a man with a metal mechanical finger hunts a woman down. When he catches her, he rapes her with the finger. She twists and cries as he pushes it in. She escapes; he hunts her down again. She is always running. He is always somewhere in the dark, coming for her.

I read them in the bright stuffy air of the parked car, where my mother leaves us while she shops for groceries on Sunday afternoons, after the Kingdom Hall meetings. My brother sleeps in the backseat. I read. I hate to be inside when she pulls the food stamps out and people stop talking to watch, to inspect what we've chosen.

When I see her wheeling the cart toward us, I slip the book back in the glove compartment and click it shut. I know the books are bad, wrong, a secret. I ask her nothing. I don't know how they fit together with the Kingdom Hall books that prohibit touching yourself, sex before marriage, oral sex, gay people. Sex with metal fingers and fathers. It's a grown-up mystery I've stumbled onto, and I feel guilty and dirty and curious.

*   *   *

In seventh grade, two other kids are in my gifted class: David Bock, who has glasses and wins Math Field Day every year, and Lisa Reddy, who raises dairy goats for 4-H. Her thick brown hair is pulled back smooth in a headband, and brown freckles cover her face and arms. She's nice to me in gifted, but not so much with her other friends. I can never tell if it's okay to sit with her in the lunchroom. Sometimes it is, and sometimes she pushes her tray away and scoots down.

In the gym after school, waiting for the bus in cold weather, kids fight. The teachers leave us alone in there with the lights off. Two boys punch each other's heads until blood spurts onto the gray bleachers.

I join the electronics club, which meets at lunch, and learn how to wire a circuit board. The club advisor is also our English teacher, as well as a minister. Each morning before school starts, he preaches on the radio, and he throws Lisa out of class when her shirt lets her obscene belly show.

One day in English he says, "How many of you girls want to go to college?" Lisa raises her hand. Tentatively — no one at home will know — I raise mine, too. "Well, stand up, you two," he says. "Everybody take a good look at these young ladies. These two want to go to college." It's a strange new feeling, a new way to think about myself. Me and Lisa, going to college.

"Do you know what college is good for in a woman?" he asks, his voice loud and strange. His face quivers, suddenly red. No one moves. "Do you know?" Everyone is quiet. "To help her raise smart *boys*." He looks around fiercely. "Boys. And that's the only thing. Do you understand me?" he yells. Everyone nods. He sighs and looks out the window.

"That's right," he says, as if to himself. "That's right," he repeats, his face cooling to its usual pale dough. He looks back at us and seems surprised to see Lisa and me still upright next to our desks. "Okay, you can sit down, girls."

*   *   *

Our friendship with the Cairns family starts when the two oldest girls, the twins Sophie and Suzanne, baby-sit for us. After the divorce, for one happy autumn, they take me under their wing. Another Witness family with a little boy invites my brother over a lot. We spend many nights away from home. It's a relief, our mother says.

I like Brother Cairns, a man my mother's age. He's an elder in our congregation, tall, lean, with a long, kind face and a voice that's low and patient. Blind from a hunting accident in his youth, he is a divorced man with custody of his three daughters and a gentle motion in his hands, living together with his white-haired mother, Mamau, as they call her, in the last little house on the left side of a gravel road that winds up a hill and ends in forest. On the right edge, the ground falls steeply down into a ravine. The Cairnses' house is covered in peeling tar paper made to look like gray brick and has a worn porch jutting out in front.

I worship the twins, eighteen. They play piano in the Kingdom Hall, Sophie especially, when we stand to sing songs from the soft-covered pink songbooks with special songs written for Witnesses, not the worldly hymns of Christendom.

Sophie is more pert, more practical and quick-tongued, while Suzanne is rangier, with higher cheekbones and cooler eyes. Her tone is lazier, more remote, as if everything she says also means, "Calm down, Sophie." But both are beautiful, with dark hair and eyes and cool, pale skin, the beauties of the Kingdom Hall.

I sleep on the lumpy fold-out couch in the living room, next to the piano where Sophie practices Kingdom Hall songs and then pounds out "Our Day Will Come" as if she's angry, her calf muscle swelling and deflating as her foot pumps the pedal. At night, I sit on their floor, watching them get ready for bed in the room they share, twin beds pushed against opposite walls with all the clutter of their lives piled or pinned nearby: curling irons, high school pennants, sheet music Sophie's learning, a football. They keep their things on their own side; if something crosses the line, they throw it back. They sleep in their bras because Marilyn Monroe did. They're seniors at the high school and worldly boys ask them out on dates, but they're waiting for good young brothers to marry.

Shelley, the younger sister, is fifteen and has gold hair instead of brown. Her eyes are lighter and thinner, but her skin is tawny and she moves with a boyish grace, like Suzanne. She sleeps in a small room with Mamau, and I think how I'd hate to share a bedroom with Nanny, who would always be telling me what to do. But they never seem to argue, and their room is as neat and quiet as a cat's licked fur.

The bathroom is small and white, with small white tiles like honeycomb and a metal heater built right into the wall. I've never seen one before, but the way its holes are curved tells me it's old. I trace my fingers around its smooth lines. The bathroom has no clutter. You could never tell it's shared by four women and a man.

There's no dining room. On the days I ride the bus home from school with Shelley, we sit at the kitchen with saucers. She spoons peanut butter onto them and then pours Hershey's syrup on top.

"Now mix it in," she says, handing me a spoon. I taste it.

"I'd thought it would be just like Reese's Peanut Butter Cups," I say, "but actually, it's better."

She laughs. "I know." We sit, our legs crossed Indian-style on the kitchen chairs, alone in the house together while Mamau's out somewhere.

When Sophie and Suzanne get home with one of their friends from the high school, we all walk over to the cemetery. The sisters' arms hang easily around each other's shoulders. We wander around, climb trees, drape ourselves backward across the tops of tombstones and let our hair hang down to the grass. We find gravestones grouped like furniture and sit like we're in a café, chatting. We talk about school and boys.

The Cairns girls are allowed to have some worldly friends; they've lived in the little house, the tiny town, their whole lives. It's natural they should know some people, Mamau says: worldly folks are just worldly, not evil. The girls make it seem possible to be a Witness and be happy.

Sometimes the four of us drive to a basketball court in one of the larger towns and meet up with older kids, the twins' age, from our Kingdom Hall. I can shoot, but I don't understand the rules, have never played in a game. I foul everyone and get in the way, annoying a boy named Greg, who tosses his blond flop of hair out of his eyes and makes wisecracks. He wishes they'd leave me home, but Suzanne says, "Come on. Cut her a break. She's just a kid." My heart surges with loyalty. I pretend they're my sisters.

Brother Cairns is always gone somewhere during the days; I never think where. In the evenings, he takes the chainsaw up the hill into the woods. Shelley positions his hands on fallen trees where the cuts need to go, and he buzzes the saw through, waiting calmly while she stacks the firewood before she returns to place his hands again. They joke with each other in soft voices. Afterward, he heads on down to the house, and we stay at the homemade basketball court, a flattened clearing of packed cinders ringed by forest, shooting baskets at a hoop he has hung on a tree. He's been blind a long time. The accident cost him his sense of smell, too, and left a dent in the side of his smooth skull that I long to put my finger in. We shoot, playing P-I-G and H-O-R-S-E as the dusk thickens and the smell of woodsmoke drifts up on the cool air from the houses down below.

After supper, we watch cop shows on the little black-and-white TV in the back room, the room they added when they built a third bedroom for Brother Cairns and that still smells of sawn wood. One of the twins narrates the action, so he can follow. Shelley doesn't do it right yet; she gets absorbed and forgets to tell him what's happening. One of them rubs his shoulders for him. The girls rub each other's backs, my back. They laugh a lot at things on television. I close my eyes and lose track of the plot.

Later, Mamau tucks me in between soft old sheets. She sits on the edge of the fold-out mattress and smooths my hair back from my forehead. I memorize her blue-sprigged housedress and the way the lines in her face all curve upward. She leaves a little green lamp on, dim, so I won't get scared. I lie between layers of faded flowers and wish I never had to go home.

When my mother comes to pick me up, she's always brisk about it, her purse tight under her arm, but something about Mamau and Brother Cairns and the offer of a cup of coffee softens her. She ends up sitting at the kitchen table with them, talking, while my brother runs in circles around the yard. I stand in the kitchen doorway, watching. When he turns toward her, Brother Cairns's face seems more open, more attentive, even more kind than it usually does. His brow wrinkles thoughtfully at things she says. He turns himself toward her like a plant toward light.

A couple of months go by and I don't say it, but one day we're in the little black Volkswagen bug she named Kizzy after watching every episode of *Roots*, even skipping meetings to see it. She's complaining about how there are no good brothers in the Clarksburg congregation to date.

"What about Brother Cairns?" I feel timid.

She glances down at me. "I had a feeling," she says. She laughs. "I think the girls are pushing that way, too."

"Well, why not?"

"What do you mean, why not? Why should I?"

"You like him, don't you? He's nice. He's an elder. I know you like him."

"It doesn't matter if I like him or not."

"How come?"

She takes a deep breath. "Well," she says slowly, "there's a rule in the Bible. I don't know if you know about it. It's a rule about getting married that people in The Truth have to follow."

"He's divorced, isn't he? Like us?"

"Yes, okay, he's divorced, but not for reasons of adultery. In the eyes of the world, he's divorced. He's legally divorced. But in the eyes of Jehovah, only adultery makes you free to get married again."

"Oh," I say, suddenly deflated. "Like Dad did."

"Yes."

"So how come Brother Cairns got divorced?"

"Well, I guess his wife had problems. They met in a school for the blind, you know, and they fell in love and got married. Had the three girls. But something went wrong with her. She started screaming a lot and getting violent—" She breaks off suddenly and glances over at me. "I don't want you to mention this over there, you hear?"

"Okay," I say quickly. "I won't."

"Don't you talk to the girls about this."

"I promise."

"Well, okay then. One night she started chasing him around the house with knives. Both of them blind. It was a danger to the girls." She drives without talking for a while. We turn off the blacktop onto our road. "It was a clear case of possession by demons." I think of my brother chasing me around the farmhouse. He was just pissed off, I decide. "And so she had to be put away."

"Put away where?"

"In a home for crazy people."

I think for a while about the crazy-people homes I've seen on TV. I wonder if the girls have to visit her there.

But my goal is to get my mother to marry him, so we can all be a family, like the Brady Bunch. *That's the way we became the Caiairns bunch,* I hum to myself in my head. The words don't fit the line. I know it's not going to happen. But dogged, I persist.

"How do they know she hasn't committed adultery with one of the crazy people?"

"Joy Elizabeth! What a thing to say." She doesn't speak for a while. "Anyway, I'm not going to marry anyone like that."

"Like what?"

94

"Someone who lives like that."

I love the way they live. "What's wrong with it?"

"All of them crammed in that tiny house, with no money coming in?" She laughs shortly. "No, thank you."

My eyes tear up. But we're home now, and we have groceries to unload.

Later, after my mother has married and we've moved away, my mother's pilot marries Suzanne, and a brother who asked me out at too young an age marries Shelley. Sophie gets no suitable offers and becomes a secretary at a law firm. The last time I see her, she's playing piano at the Kingdom Hall as we sing "The Shulamite Maiden," her brow furrowed, her mouth pursed, her high-heeled foot furiously pumping.

"Dog! Hey, dog!" It's eighth grade. Something hits me in the back. Soft. Dirt probably. Then a stick. *Dog* is what kids call me. I'm sitting on the grassy hill of the old brick middle school, reading, waiting for Mrs. McCarthy to come out of the library. She's the librarian, my homeroom teacher, and the advisor of the school paper, which meets at lunch, so I can write for it. She lives farther on down our road, and the school bus takes an hour, so sometimes she lets me ride home with her, watches from the window of her red Cherokee Chief as I get out and walk to the door. Sometimes she suggests books she thinks I'd like. She is tall and plump, with curly brown hair and glasses, and older than my mother, who bakes cakes for Mrs. McCarthy's brother-in-law, our school bus driver, and stands in the road talking to him. He's married. I hate the way my mother goes out and chats with him, hand on hip, jaunty, tilting her face up. But we're the last kids on his run; the bus is empty, so the delay is no problem, he says.

"Hey, dog!" A rock hits my neck, but I can tell without reaching up to touch it that the skin's not broken. No one says my name.

I have my brother to play with, but there is a certain amount of loneliness. My mother doesn't take me to the Cairnses' anymore, and there aren't any other Witnesses in our town. In school, the girls cluster together, gelling into little groups that break apart and form again differently.

From issues of *Seventeen* and my mother's old *New Woman* magazines I clip photographs of girls and women and glue them into a red spiral notebook, one to a page. Underneath, I write what their relationship is to me: older sister, friend, cousin. I write long descriptions, making up their names, ages, and hobbies.

A pretty woman in a flannel shirt kneels in her garden, smiling at me over the spade in her gloved hands, wisps of pale hair twirling out from under her scarf, the ad for vitamins cut away. I write that she is my young aunt, who has no children of her own and loves to take me out for ice cream.

A girl my age with long red hair and a back-to-school tartan skirt swings gaily from a parking meter on a pretty street lined with trees and brownstones. My best friend. We walk to school together in the mornings. I fill a whole notebook with made-up friends.

8

For the two years my mother is married to my stepfather, I do not grow. When they wed on the Ides of March, 1980, I am twelve years old, five feet six inches tall. When I run away in the snowy dark, I am fourteen years old and still five six. I've dropped sixteen pounds. My cheeks and hipbones jut. My face is gaunt. When I get food again, I grow two inches more.

During those two years, my brother has cavities so bad he cries in class. His third grade teacher sends him to the cafeteria to pack salt into his teeth. Our mother does nothing, takes him to no dentists. Our stepfather beats him with a belt each day, and kicks him in the head. Our mother does nothing. Sometimes, she weeps. Then our stepfather beats her, shoves her up against the wall of the trailer after a Kingdom Hall meeting, her little high heels dangling. He bloodies her nose and mouth, and spits great gobs of saliva in her face as we watch from the doorway. It runs down her jaw, the blood mixing in like little pink threads.

He is savage, huge, with pale blue eyes, thin lips, a bald head, a huge paunch matted with hair, and thick fists with black hair crawling onto the fingers.

Mutual Kingdom Hall friends introduce them. He comes to

dinner one evening when my friend Tammy is sleeping over. At the table, she leans to whisper, "Mother, father, and all my children." She smirks, winks.

"No," I whisper back. They're talking to each other, not paying attention to us. I'm suddenly angry and afraid. I thought he was just one more Witness to fill the big bare table, like the pioneers, or Betty and her two dumb kids, or retarded Annie Lou, who spat food when she talked.

"Why not?"

I glare at her.

Later, closed in my room, she asks why again. "Your mom obviously needs to get married, and he's a brother."

"Maybe she does, but not him."

"But *why*?"

I struggle to put it into words, and fail. "He has fishy eyes." It's true. The flesh around them is static, even when the rest of his face smiles or frowns. Their pale blue has no depth or warmth.

"Fishy eyes? Fishy *eyes*?" She rolls with laughter on my bed. "You're crazy. Fishy eyes. Geez."

But there's something wrong. I smell it on him like a dog smells fear.

He gives my brother Tonka trucks and me the radio I crave. He buys my mother clothes and me a plum velvet blazer, very grown up, for wearing to the Kingdom Hall. "Won't it be nice," my mother purrs, "to use the child support your father sends just on school clothes and nice things, instead of bills?"

She's got us there. I'm sick of food stamps, government cheese, and clothes discarded by strangers. Middle school is a bad time to be poor. And I'm tall for my age. At assemblies, eighteen-year-old brothers from other congregations flirt with me between sessions, ask my mother if they can take me out. They back away, apologizing, when they learn I'm only twelve. I want a black leather clutch purse and combs for my hair. But not this way. I argue with her, but things move quickly. He makes fourteen dollars an hour working construction, she says. He's a respected brother; he's served at Bethel, the Watchtower headquarters in Brooklyn, where all our books and magazines are printed. A date is set. I'm to wear my plum velvet blazer. My brother, seven, is to give her away in the ceremony at our Kingdom Hall.

"Won't that be cute?" she says.

"No, not really," I say.

I cry in her room as she dresses, begging her not to do it, but I have no evidence aside from the weird way he looks at us.

She's patient for a while, reminding me again of the money he makes, the good reputation he has in the congregation, but finally she turns on me.

"I am just about fed up, you hear? Do you understand me? I've just about had it with your bellyaching." She swings the hairbrush in my face. "Why do you always want to ruin everything? *Why?* One good thing comes along, something that will actually make me happy for once, and you have to start your whining."

"He's not a good man." I'm still crying. She laughs angrily, throws the brush down on the bureau.

"What do you know about good men? You're twelve years old." Her voice is rich with disgust. "Do you think you know what a good man is? Do you?" She grabs and shakes me. "Well?" I just cry. "Do you think your *father's* a good man?" I look at the brown-and-green carpet, nodding. She stares at me, then looses me with a final shake and turns her back. She steps into the silky fawn dress. "Well, that just shows what you know."

It's early in the day, but the wide straps of her bra are already gouging into her shoulders, scoring the red welts I see when she changes into her nightgown at night. She tosses her head, talks to the mirror. "You listen here. I'm getting married today, and there's nothing, absolutely nothing, that you can do about it. Do you hear me?"

"Yes."

"For your information, young lady, I am happy. You can be happy, too, or you can sit in the corner and snivel. Is that clear?"

"Yes."

When the elder asks, "Who gives this woman in marriage?" my brother, confused, must be prodded to speak.

"I do," he says, worried, his eyes casting about to see if he's done the right thing.

There is no honeymoon. They sleep in my bedroom, where my mother has moved her furniture; she doesn't want to sleep in the same room where she slept with my father. All my furniture is in their room, my room now, its light blue carpet no good as grass. Now my bed is a ship, carrying my horses to somewhere over the sea.

The morning after the wedding, I wake to go to the bathroom. As soon as I enter the hall, our stepfather appears, wearing only his underwear, loose grayed briefs. It shocks me; I've never seen him except fully dressed in Kingdom Hall clothes. My father is the only man I've ever seen in underwear, bright psychedelic briefs he bought stacks of in London.

He steps in front of me, his legs massive, his hairy paunch jutting like the belly of a pregnant woman. I'm used to feeling tall, but he towers over me, and in my nightgown I am frightened and young. I move aside to pass him, and he steps in front of me. His dark nipples prick my eyes. There's no way around. We stand like this for seconds. I look up into his face, finally, and a grin slides across it like oil. He laughs. Then he steps aside. I rush into the bathroom, shut the door, and shove the bolt home. From the hallway, he laughs again.

Our grandmother, our mother's kindly mother — not a Witness — has been for years a sort of fairy godmother. I love her fluffed white hair and freckled arms. When we've visited her in Waukegan, she takes me out to lunch at a big department store, just the two of us.

All afternoon we meander through the racks together; I get to show her which things I like. She buys a little tweed suit and a white linen dress with thin purple ribbons — one too old for me, the other too extravagant, my mother says.

From her has come the money for my bedroom furniture, "the kind of furniture a young lady should have," maple dressers and a double bed, a nightstand with thin spooled legs. From her has come our organ, on which I take lessons, the metronome swinging its click. I long for a piano, though. It takes me months to write her, I'm so afraid of hurting her feelings.

"Of course," she replies right away. I'm to ask my mother to sell the organ and use the money to buy me a piano. We sell the organ easily, and my mother puts the money in a savings account in my name. I scour the classifieds for a used piano. I want one just like the Cairnses', an upright with scratches and curly carvings.

But after she marries my stepfather and tells him about it, he wants the money. I refuse to take it out. This goes on for days, him pressing at every interchange, me refusing.

"The money is from my grandmother. It's for a piano. It's not for you." He wants it to pay some debts. "What happened to all this money you were supposed to make working construction, anyway?" He yells and bullies, asks what kind of an ingrate brat my mother's raising, what kind of a smart-ass. After a few days, my mother begins to press me, too. We can always buy a piano later, she says. I hold out for a while. She gets angrier. I sign the little slip, and they go to the bank.

The promised wealth does not materialize. Our stepfather visits numerous doctors until one agrees to sign the papers that say he has black lung, so the government will support him.

He wants our mother at home, caring for him and for the house, like an obedient, dutiful wife. She sells her half of the furniture business to her partner, who is worried for her. But my stepfather insists. He's going to get this women's lib stuff right out of her, get her back in the house where she belongs, in submission to her husband as the congregation is in submission to the Lord. It's not Christian, the way she carries on.

He doesn't like my brother and me, calls us snotty. He doesn't like the way we say *Please* and *Thank you* — like little rich kids, he says. He doesn't like the way we look him in the eye. *Sir,* we are to call him.

The first disability check arrives. He stops working, stays home, swigs great gulps of prescription cough medicine straight from the bottle, his eyes glassy. He's constantly there, watching.

Shortly after the wedding, Buddy starts to lose weight. He's a young dog, but suddenly he looks tired, and the skin around his eyes wrinkles up. His nose gets warm.

"We need to take him to the vet," I say. My stepfather's face hardens.

"Vets are expensive," my mother says, glancing at him. "Let's give it another week, wait and see."

We give it another week, and then another. Buddy limps from one spot to another on the porch and then lies still, whimpering. I hold his head on my lap until it gets dark. Inside, I plead, "When are we going to take him to the vet? He's only getting worse."

"Will you just shut up about the dog already?" my stepfather yells, rising from a chair. His belly shakes inside the T-shirt. My eyes come up to his chest.

"If he's sick and we don't take him, it's the same as killing him. We'd be murderers. And if you're the one who doesn't let us, then you'd be the murderer."

"What did you say to me?" he roars. My mother slips between us.

"You just watch your mouth, young lady," she says quickly, her tone sharp, glancing his way. "You think twice before you say a thing like that. Just who do you think you are?" Behind her, he subsides.

Buddy dies one day while we're at school and is buried before we get home.

*   *   *

We are used to the emptiness of the farmhouse when we get home from school: for the last two years, our mother has always been at work. Our habit has been to settle in front of the television for our two shows, *The Brady Bunch* and *My Three Sons*, fractured, makeshift families where the adults solve the kids' problems with a laugh and a pat on the shoulder. Then homework, dinner, baths, and bed. But now our stepfather is there when we get off the bus, waiting with lists of chores for us, endless tasks we cannot finish before dark.

One day, I say we are tired.

His chuckle sounds like coins shaking in a metal box. "You think I care any more about you than that damn dog?" he says. We look at him. He grins. "Watch and learn," he says. "You get to work."

He forbids me to sing, except at the Kingdom Hall. Caught, I am beaten with the belt.

As planned, my father and stepmother take us to Key West for our visit, a whole week. Our cousins are there, and everything is just like it usually is, like all the years before, but a sense of dread hangs over things now. My father's jokes aren't funny. I'm not hungry when Nanny calls us to the table, to the garlic roast pork and *papas rellenos,* her home-made black beans and saffron rice. The cousins and their games seem childish; the beach is just a lot of sand. When Papi cries his good-bye, I cry, too, feeling that I'll never see him again.

When we return home, my mother and stepfather have sold the farmhouse. They've bought a mobile home, fourteen by sixty feet, off-white corrugated metal with brown trim.

Our mother's ridicule, the way she beats my brother with objects, has seemed normal to us. All the brothers and sisters see, and no one is perturbed. "I love you," she tells us every night, tucking us in, and we know she does: at other times she holds us, reads us stories, pets our hair, and calls us little nicknames.

This is different. Our stepfather is a stranger, malevolent, and our mother doesn't seem to notice. He yells that we are clumsy, stupid. He does not call my brother by his name; he calls him *boy, idiot, dummy, clumsy*. I am *girl* — if he's in a good mood, *girly*.

On the visitation weekend, I ask my father if he can get custody of us. He says yes, of course he will.

When the papers are served, our stepfather says it's just fine with him if we go to our father's to live — if we want to turn our backs on Jehovah, on God's law, if we want to be apostates, antichrists, if we want to be cast into the fires of Gehenna, he couldn't care less. He doesn't want us in his house, doesn't want us around, even though our mother does, he says, but that's because she's stupid. A couple of spoiled brats who don't know how to work. Our mother stands aside, head bowed, hands clasped, tears drooling down her cheeks. But we move to a trailer park in a town hours away, in an area even more rural. We will start new schools in the fall.

In the trailer park, kids gather in the road outside to hear him yell at our mother. The sound goes right through the metal. At the bus stop, they tease us about it.

The money problems worsen. Our clothes are not replaced. We start the new school shabby, in castoffs. If we want clothes for school, he tells us, we can have a yard sale, sell our toys. Our mother urges us: we'll feel so much better if we have some nice things.

All Saturday we sit in the small grass rectangle that is the trailer's rented yard. Strange kids pick up my horse models, Tony's Matchbox cars and Tonka trucks. One by one the items go, my family of gray Arabians scattered.

We make almost a hundred dollars, we show them proudly at the end of the day. It can buy new shoes for both of us, new pants, maybe some sweaters.

My stepfather takes the stacks of ones from my hand. There will be no clothes. Everything that's ours, he says, is his. Get used to it.

We go to school ragged, mismatched, hopeless.

*   *   *

Because he has married our mother, because he is a dedicated brother in the Kingdom Hall, because he has lived and worked at Bethel — the ultimate sign of spiritual devotion — and because our own father is disfellowshipped, it should be plain to us that he is our spiritual father now. He sits on the leather sofa that our parents bought in England, our mother silent next to him. We sit across from him on the trailer's stiff orange carpet.

He is our father now, our spiritual father. He says it again and again. He points to scriptures, rustling his fingers through the thin pages of his Bible. We've been sitting here for hours, and it's my fault. I won't say he is my father.

"I am your spiritual father. The head of this household." Our mother nods each time he speaks. Her eyes are red and tired.

"I'm sorry," I say. I was raised to be completely obedient, perfectly respectful to all authority, all adults. But I was also raised never to lie. "You're not my father."

"Will you just *say* it?" whispers Tony, fighting tears. I'm the one making us sit here. I don't want him to cry. I can't stand the crumpled look of fear on his little face.

"I won't call you father," I say again and again. I grasp at straws. "My father has black hair. My parents are divorced. You're not my father. You talk about God, but God hates a liar."

I won't, I won't, I won't. Over and over, I refuse. How his eyes gleam each time I say I won't.

9

Two scriptures change our lives.

1 Corinthians 5:9–11:
> In my letter I wrote you to quit mixing in company with fornicators, not meaning entirely with the fornicators of this world or the greedy persons and extortioners or idolaters. Otherwise, you would actually have to get out of the world. But now I am writing you to quit mixing in company with anyone called a brother that is a fornicator or a greedy person or an idolater or a reviler or a drunkard or an extortioner, not even eating with such a man.

2 John 9–11:
> Everyone that pushes ahead and does not remain in the teaching of the Christ does not have God. He that does remain in this teaching is the one that has both the Father and the Son. If anyone comes to you and does not bring this teaching, never receive him into your homes or say a greeting to him. For he that says a greeting to him is a sharer in his wicked works.

Our stepfather explains them to us. We are no longer to speak to our father, not even to say hello, and we are not to break bread with him. We must go on visitations, because that is the law — we render Caesar's things unto Caesar, as Christ commanded — unless we can persuade our father to give us up. He is an apostate, a disfellowshipped person, worse than a worldly person, for he has known The Truth and rejected it, preferring Satan's ways. He must be shunned. We may not greet him or speak to him at all. *Not even eating with such a man.* And he cannot come into the house when he picks us up. These are the rules now, our stepfather tells us, the proper understanding of scripture, which our mother has been too lax and lazy to enforce. This is what true Witnesses do.

That's ridiculous, I say. We've been eating with him and talking to him for five years since he was disfellowshipped, and nobody at the Kingdom Hall ever said a thing about it. Our mother let us. Our mother talks to him all the time.

"Not anymore," says our stepfather.

We go to our father's house for the weekend, and I tell him about the weird new rules. We act like we normally do. It won't be long, he tells us, and this will be all over; we'll be living with him. His lawyer says it's open and shut.

When we get back to the mobile home, our stepfather sits us down, our overnight bags still in our hands, and questions us. We tell the truth: of course we spoke and ate with our father.

Our stepfather beats us with his belt. He will beat it out of us, he says, this spirit of rebellion. As long as we are under his roof, he is responsible for our spiritual well-being. He cannot condone sin. He must reprove it with the rod.

It is, after all, what we believe in. "Need for Mental Cleansing," reads a subheading in the *1970 Yearbook of Jehovah's Witnesses*: "It is evident, therefore, that there must be a cleaning out of the mind if there is to be an implanting of right thinking."

Each visitation weekend becomes a terror. We return home to interrogations, beatings with our pants down until our legs buckle and he yells at us to get up so he can finish, scriptures yelled aloud for endless hours, our mother on the couch remote as a mannequin. Each time we go to our father's, we talk less.

And then, abruptly, almost mysteriously, we give in, and we do so with gusto. We believe our stepfather's dictates and obey them. On visitations, we won't eat with our father or talk to him. We hum or whistle when he speaks to us. When he pleads with me, I roll my eyes.

As soon as we get into his car, I fall asleep. When I wake up at his house, long red welts have broken out on my forearms. Stress, our stepmother says. The welts last for the weekend and then melt away to clean skin.

As punishment for speaking to our father on previous visits, my brother and I have to copy out chapters from the Watchtower books; they'd better be finished when we return to the trailer. We copy them longhand into notebooks in our rooms. I fall asleep whenever I'm not moving. I cannot stay awake. Stress, our stepmother says, shaking her pretty blond head, her eyes sad and angry.

Our stepfather orders me to keep a log of every moment and turn it in to him when we return. My notes must be valid in a court of law, he says, and they must record our activities minute by minute. I try, dating them: *Friday, January the 30th, 1981 A.D.* I write in the third person: *At 8:45 p.m., Joy got into her nightclothes, after crocheting and reading the Evolution book, and went to bed.* When I mention my father, I put it in quotation marks: *our "father."*

On Saturday nights, I have to call our stepfather to report on our activities. Have we watched worldly movies, mingled with worldly friends of our father? Have we gone to a worldly art museum? Have we spoken or eaten with him who has become unclean?

Our father is frantic. He talks to his lawyer, to a child psychologist. "My children behave as if they are autistic," he writes. He cries to us. "Look how you're *hurting* me," he says. "Do you want to hurt your father?" My stomach knots and twists, but I cannot look at him. He tries getting angry, says that this is not how he has raised us to behave. I write notes that say I must be obedient to Jehovah.

We are mute. He asks us to blink once for no, twice for yes. We blink, not meeting his eyes, catatonic with faith. When we call from the Kingdom Hall for a ride home, one cough means no, two mean yes.

For months, we obey our stepfather's rules. Our father submits letter after letter to the lawyers, documenting the way we no longer speak to him, look at him, do what he asks, documenting the way our stepfather yells at him, threatens, when he arrives to pick us up. (In my father's hand: *He threatens to have my arm or leg broken. "I got cousins in Pittsburgh. Anything I want, like ordering it off a menu."* Another day: *"I wish you'd break into my house. Come on. Break into my house. Because then I could really take care of you."*)

In the trailer, my brother and I may walk and be only in certain places. We can be in our own bedrooms. We can walk down the little hallway that goes to our rooms, but we cannot be in the hallway together: we must wait until the hallway is empty to walk. We can be in the bathroom at the end of the hall, our bathroom, but we cannot be in it together, even if we are just brushing our teeth. We cannot enter each other's rooms.

To get to the kitchen — where we are allowed only for meals and chores — there is a specific diagonal path across the living room that we may follow, where the orange rug is mashed down, between the octagonal coffee table and the television.

We may not pause. We may not glance at the television if it is on. We may not sit on the couch, unless it is family Bible study — Monday, Wednesday, and Saturday nights — to prepare for meetings on the following days.

During Bible study, we seldom read the Bible. We read articles in the *The Watchtower* for Sunday mornings, other articles for Thursday nights, and sections of various Watchtower Society books for the book-study on Tuesday evenings. All the same size, all with plain spines — on the shelf, you can tell them apart only by color. *Did Man Get Here by Evolution or Creation?* Light blue. *Life Does Have a Purpose,* red. Dull green: *Making Your Family Life Happy.*

The sectional couch is tan leather, tufted, with leather-covered buttons. It had looked strange in the old farmhouse, the living room with its walls of bare log and white mud, the original log cabin that the farmhouse was built up around. Now the sofa's three sleek pieces curve on the mobile-home rug that still stinks of formaldehyde. I sit with a book or magazine open on my lap, fingering the rectangular leather patch that covers our father's cigarette burn, over which our mother had yelled and cried. His carelessness, which ruined everything.

Our stepfather tells my mother or me to read the numbered paragraphs; his own reading was so poor that my brother and I would glance at each other, so he beat us, and read no more. After each paragraph, he asks the numbered questions printed at the bottom of the page. We underline the answers in our texts. We raise our hands. He calls on us. He addresses my mother by the long and formal version of her name. It sounds strange; my father always used her nickname, the one her friends call her. My stepfather sounds like he is talking to a child, like she has misbehaved in some way, or like he doesn't know her.

If he calls on us, we read the line or phrase from the paragraph that answers the printed question. There is no discussion. We move to the next paragraph. It is just like the meetings, only with no microphones carried up and down the aisles by young brothers, and no smiling or chatting afterward. When it's over, we return to our rooms alone.

We can sit in our chairs at the kitchen table in the kitchen during meals. I can stand at the sink, because I wash the dishes every night. We cannot open the refrigerator or any cupboards.

Beyond the kitchen lies the great unknown, the half-remembered, for we were only allowed there once, when we returned from Key West to find that the farmhouse had been sold, the mobile home purchased. We walked through its metal shell, numb, fascinated by the master bath's round tub, big enough for a family. So we know that beyond the kitchen lies a hallway with folding doors that open to reveal a washer and dryer, that a back door leads outside to a five-foot drop down to dirt. At the end is a bedroom as wide as the trailer itself, and then the astonishing bathroom. But we do not go there. We may not step past the edge of the kitchen linoleum. When it's time to clean the house on Saturdays, my mother wheels the vacuum cleaner out of some unknown closet and pushes its handle toward me.

One visitation weekend, our father's wife comes into my room with my brother and me. She sits down on the floor and faces us, squeezing her hands together, her blue eyes anxious.

"Has your father ever been anything but decent and loving to you?"

"No." When our father speaks, we are to whistle or hum. But we can answer her, if we try to keep it to one word — one syllable, if possible.

"Then how can you treat him like this? Don't you know how terrible you're making him feel?"

"Yes."

Though not an apostate herself, she loves an apostate and is worldly. Still, it's hard to be firm around her. She's sweet and sad and gentle. Her hands are light and soft when she strokes our hair, and she never criticizes us. When we make a mistake, she just shows us how to do it right. She believes children are born innocent, not in original sin. She loves art museums and paints horses on big canvases and buys us bottles of bubbles. Once we sat on the porch of their garage apartment and blew bubbles together all afternoon, sprawled on the hammock, the porch swing, the four of us.

Now she takes notes on our behavior for the lawyer because she can be more objective, because my father cannot bear to: "The children are rude and disobedient."

The town where our stepfather has moved us is a small college town, but we do not go to the campus. We do not attend cultural events or lectures. We go witnessing house-to-house in the neighborhoods around the college, where students answer the doors hungover on weekends, and I peer around them at the interesting posters and lava lamps.

The college admissions materials describe the town's atmosphere as "quaint." A few years after we live there, it will be included in *The 100 Best Small Towns in America.*

He is going to beat my brother for some miniscule infraction. Something unbelievable, unpreventable, something insane. Tony is trembling, his eyes wide and drawn.

"Beat me instead," I say. Our stepfather's eyebrows rise, and his blue eyes widen. A grin begins to swirl upward in the corner of his mouth. "I'll take his beating."

"You hear that, Mother?" he says. "She wants to get beat for the dummy." Our mother stands in the kitchen behind the room divider, looking through its wooden spindles at the orange carpet where we stand. "You think I ought to allow that?"

There's a pause. "It's her decision," she says.

"All right," he says. "Get over here, girl." I pull my pants down, bend over, and grip the edge of the coffee table.

He beats me with his belt. Hard, until my legs give out, and I'm gasping onto the glass.

"What do you think of that?" he says. "Feel like a hero, do you?"

And then he beats my brother, too.

* * *

I am a tall woman, fine-featured, dark-eyed, dark-haired. My shoulders are broad. I am large-boned, taller than some men. To look at me, you would imagine I was strong, invulnerable. Someone who could protect herself, who could protect others, who could have done so then.

Our father, desperate, composes a lengthy letter to the Watchtower Bible and Tract Society in Brooklyn, detailing the four custody hearings in 1980, his conversations with congregation elders, and the new policy of our stepfather: "that the Bible teaches that children must not associate with their disfellowshipped father, to the extent of: *not eating with him, not speaking to him, not listening to him, not obeying him or in any way having anything to do with the disfellowshipped parent* with whom the children do not reside. We love each other very much, but they now believe that they must treat me as if I were dead.

"The local news media is interested in this very controversial court case, and it may be advisable for the Watch Tower Society to be prepared to comment on this issue." Already the hearings have been in the paper, a local curiosity: a mother's rights, the issue of religious freedom. It is 1980, and the judge is old. He believes children should always go with their mother, unless she is blatantly unfit — a drug addict, not just a religious fundamentalist. He doesn't want to tangle with it. Freedom of religion is what this country's based on.

"I am asking for your assistance in this matter, hoping that a clarification by you will allow my children and me to once again enjoy the loving, close relationship we enjoyed until recently."

A bland response arrives two weeks later. It acknowledges no role, shifting all responsibility instead onto the local congregations. All the elders can do, it says, is give appropriate counsel. If my mother and stepfather do not see fit to comply with the counsel, then there really is not much more that the elders can do. As to whether my father should continue the legal efforts that he has undertaken, this of course is something that he would have to decide. Since the issue is somewhat of a personal or family matter, it will be up to him to choose what he feels is the best way to handle it. The letter is rubber-stamped, not signed: *Watchtower B. + T. Society* in an angular cursive, as though it had been patterned on the handwriting of a real person once, and, below it, *of New York, Inc.* in tiny square-cut capitals.

Months go by this way. We refuse to eat with him, talk to him, or acknowledge he exists. We walk like wooden figures from the door of his house to our rooms, closing ourselves in until it's time to go out in service or to the Kingdom Hall.

One weekend, on the drive back to the trailer, my father pulls the car to the side of the road. He turns around in his seat to face us. I look out the window. He tells us that the child psychologist believes that the visitations, in their current state, are doing more harm than good. Our father has prepared for the judge a list of reasons why the visitations have ceased to be meaningful. He reads it to us. It is an enumeration of everything bad we have done. For these reasons, he says, he will no longer be coming to pick us up. It's what we wanted, it's what we worked for, and now we have it. He won't see us anymore. Perhaps in the future, things will change; we might change our minds. The court must take our opinions into account when we turn fourteen. Until then, this is the end. The end of seeing our father, indefinitely. Do we have anything we'd like to say?

We do not. My throat is thick, but I don't look at him. He sighs, faces front, and turns the key in the ignition. His wife reaches over to hold his hand.

When we're back in the trailer, we tell our stepfather and mother. He pats our shoulders. We have triumphed for Jehovah, he says. We have overcome the wicked one, broken the spirit of Satan. We should be very proud.

Later, my mother receives a letter from the lawyer. "Huh," she says, reading it to herself in the kitchen. "Looks like your father's getting out of paying child support, too." She turns to us. "How do you like that, kids?" She says it loudly, so our stepfather can hear over the TV. I think, *It's a performance for him. She has to do it.* "Just goes to show you what he really cares about." *She doesn't mean to hurt us.*

Now we see no one. We go to the school, where we are new, and the Kingdom Hall, a white clapboard one-room building, where no one knows us yet.

When the weather warms up and school has ended, they move the mobile home from the trailer park to an unimproved piece of land, forty-eight forested acres with no utilities, twelve miles outside the small town. They do not send our father the new address. He has no idea where we are.

Our grandmother, kind but never close, has drifted out of our lives, pacified by our mother's letters and chirpy voice on the phone, alienated by her strangeness, her religiosity.

There is no one to care about us. No friends, no relatives, few neighbors on the dirt road carved back into the mountains.

10

On the trailer walls hang his enlarged toadstools and wildflowers, all framed in brown plastic molded to look like woodland branches. He's made money, he tells us, on his photographs in the past. His butterflies, a foot wide, perch on milkweed pods, one drop of dew glimmering.

He shoots portraits of my brother and me against a black background. He gets out white umbrellas and sets up everything in the living room.

"Your girl's photogenic," he tells my mother.

He loves to photograph me.

At the park, the forest is quiet around us. There is only the crickets' purr rising and falling in the hot afternoon, only the click and whir of his Nikon as he circles me, only his murmurs telling me how to shift my limbs. Somewhere close there is a lake, but I cannot see it. The park is deserted on weekdays during summer vacation, when he takes me there. No cars are in the parking lot when we arrive or leave.

He unties the little straps of my halter top and lets them fall, shooting my shoulders, collarbones, grunting approval.

"These are getting in the way," he says, and I stare at the Nikon on its strap, its closed eye resting on the upper crest of his gut, as his fingers stuff the fabric straps inside the upper edge of my shirt. He backs away again, tilts his head.

"Better."

They are not my mother's idea, these modeling sessions, but she approves, parroting his words: it's a way for us to become better acquainted, so I won't be so tense around him.

On the way to the park, that first time, he tells me to unbuckle my seatbelt and slide across next to him. When I hesitate, he reaches across my lap to cup my thigh and drags me sudden and tight against his huge body, his arm going hard around my shoulders, his fingers curled, his little finger resting at the top of my breast as though by accident or oversight.

"You're my little girl, now, aren't you? Daddy's little girl. My little girly girl. All mine, all mine. You're Daddy's little girl now, aren't you?"

I do not have to answer yes or no. His talk is an unbroken stream, guttural, breathless.

My mother has told me to be affectionate, that he just wants to learn to be a good father. I let him squeeze me, my shoulder, my thigh. In his grip, I stare out at the blurred scenery rushing past.

I am really that running dog on the side of the road. I am those children leaping from the porch, laughing. I am actually that evergreen tree. I am not speeding forward in this vehicle, clamped tight against a muttering stranger.

During another session, he looms in again, his lips curled, baring his small yellow teeth.

"Listen, I know what we can do to really get your mom. This will drive her crazy," he says. Later, I will learn that he has married other women with pubescent daughters. They were blond. He will show us slides.

"I don't want to drive her crazy."

"Oh, come on. Every teenage girl wants to get her mother." He grins. "She'll go nuts when she sees this." His furred hands reach for my chest, and I freeze. He pulls the top of my shirt down, tug by tug, until only my nipples are covered. "This'll definitely get her." He chuckles, backing away with his camera cocked. "Make her think we're out here taking nudie pictures, huh?"

I stare at the tops of trees, thinking how the light is fading, how odd it is to be alone with him in the darkening forest. He tells me to smile, but I can't.

"Okay. Well, that's good, then. Yeah. That moody type look."

The camera clicks and clicks. I am really that black crow flying over, heading for the lake.

Our mother mails photographs of us in a blithe, cheery, scripture-quoting letter to her old business partner at the furniture store, who immediately calls our father.

"The kids look like they're in a concentration camp," she tells him. The photos scare her. We've lost weight, we're pale, our eyes have dark circles under them, our smiles are stiff and frightened. She says the shots of me in the forest are alarming — she can't tell exactly what's going on, but they sure show a lot of skin.

She offers to testify in court on our father's behalf. She registers a complaint with the elders in our old congregation, where she still goes.

But nothing happens.

It is the straightness and elegance of my hand that has landed me the task, the lean fineness of my lettering, so different from my stepfather's blunt wavering scrawl, all capital letters — like the writing of a convict, I think.

White paint on blue metal. I time myself: it takes eight seconds to pass the brush swiftly in four strokes, to form two seagulls gliding in the door's corner, above and to the right of *FARM USE*. I count so if he asks, "What are you doing wasting time?" I can say, "It only took eight seconds." The birds are an afterthought, a last-minute touch, just something to make it a little special, a little pretty. But now that he's coming across the field in the dusk, I am afraid. But he does not ask. He glares at me where I'm crouched by the truck wheel. "Artistic," he sneers. He spits a wad of phlegm at the driveway, where it lands and spreads, a dark moistening ring in the dust. It's late now, getting dark; he doesn't make me scrape them off. He heads for the trailer and his pie. Squatting in the dirt, I breathe, and my fingers loosen on the brush.

In rural areas, the occasional truck has *FARM USE* painted on its sides, a special dispensation to relieve the small family farm from the expenses of a license and insurance.

In the back, sometimes, gaunt children ride, their arms wrapped tiredly around their knees, hunched amid hay bales or firewood or piles of metal scrap. They stare dead-eyed into the car behind.

Our stepfather drives our *FARM USE* truck all over town: the post office, the grocery. Tony and I sit in the back, staring at children belted safely into seats beside their parents. Sometimes, they're children from school, children we know. They point, talk to their parents excitedly, stare at us in fascination and disgust.

I begin to feel I am an animal. I begin to feel I am insane.

Our hair maddens him. From five yards, he can spot a stray strand of dark hair flopped sideways over the regulation part that now scalps my brother in half at all times. Our stepfather can see a crooked part from across a field — calls it, judge and judgment, even as the leather starts sliding through his loops, as my brother's face crumples and goes numb.

My hair, he says, needs to get out of my face, out of my eyes. It's long and straight and dark. He can't see my expression, he says, and that's a disrespectful, ungodly way for a girl to look, hanging her hair over her face, looking through it like a curtain. My mother has thrown down a rare barrier: he can no longer beat me. Perhaps something about my body, bent in its underwear, disturbs her. He finds other ways to punish me.

I can pin my hair back with barrettes, or I can have it cut by my mother, my bangs clipped short at the hairline to show my forehead. I pull it back and secure it with plastic combs.

One day, we've gone out in service after a Sunday morning meeting. Everyone behaves. My mother obeys him. But when we get back to the trailer, he begins bellowing as if he's gone mad.

"Get me the scissors!" he yells at her, pushing me into my room. Unquestioning, she brings them, still confused, and he snatches them from her. "I've had just about enough out of you, girly!" he yells, shoving me backward.

"What did I do?" I'm crying.

He pushes me down on the bed, towering over me, his legs spread on either side of mine. My brother has gone to his room, crying, afraid of what's happening, but more afraid to break the rule that bars him from my room. A tendril has slipped out and blown across my forehead. My stepfather yanks on it, shoves it in front of my eyes.

"You think you're gonna get away with this bullshit?"

One hand is huge in the center of my chest, pinning me down, and the other tears the combs away from my scalp and throws them on the bed. The cool blades sweep my forehead, and I feel the soft scatter of hair as it falls onto my face and slips off. He hovers there, breathing heavily, his eyes small.

"That takes care of that," he says finally, rising off me. My mother, crying, follows him down the hall. When their bedroom door closes, I go to the bathroom mirror. A fringe juts out ugly near my hairline.

My mother's hair goes uncut, uncolored. It grows out a wiry gray, straggling around her shoulders. A woman's beauty is within, he says when she asks for money for dye. Jehovah doesn't care what she looks like. If she would just learn to obey, in perfect meekness as Paul commanded, then her price would be more than rubies.

He forbids her to wear makeup. All at once, her face looks old and tired.

My ass is a moving target. That's what he calls it, *ass*, a word we're not allowed to say. I cannot pass the couch without a slap, a pinch, a long stroke that ends in squeezing. I walk as quickly, straightly, as invisibly as I can.

"This girl of yours sure does love to wiggle, don't she, Mother?" he calls to the kitchen.

"Yes, she does," comes a deadened voice.

As time passes, the rules intensify. Food becomes a measured thing. Each mealtime, my stepfather dishes himself up from the pots. My mother may take half of his helping size for herself. Then, while he watches, she can spoon half of her portion size onto my plate, and half of that goes to my brother. If my stepfather wants one peanut butter and jelly sandwich, my brother gets one-eighth. If she gives us more than my stepfather calculates is correct, he beats Tony with his belt.

We sit at dinner, our eyes on our plates. If we look our stepfather in the eye, ever, without being told, we're beaten.

"How those little titties of yours doing?" he says to me. "They must be sprouting pretty good right about now."

If I do not keep eating, I'll have stomach pains later, or I'll have to eat dry the packets of Carnation Instant Breakfast we all got free in gym and which the other girls leave lying in their lockers. After class, I try to make my voice casual. "Are you going to eat that?" I say, pointing.

They look at each other, grinning. Then back at me, their eyes cool and repelled. "No. My God. Take it if you want it."

You're supposed to pour it in milk, but I have no milk. On the school bus, I sink down so no one can see me and rip the top back, pour the dry grains in my mouth, chew. I learn to like it.

"Must be like two puppies. Isn't that right, Mother?"

"Yes."

"Two puppies with brown noses."

Something in my throat is clogging, but I chew, eyes down, head down. My brother keeps eating. I feel my mother's gaze like a beam of heat in my hair.

We are not allowed into the grocery store, or any store. We are forbidden from going to the post office. We cannot touch money. There are no trips to the movie theater, the mall, or the park. We are prohibited, now, from even visiting Witnesses, unless our stepfather is there with us. He is always there, watching.

I begin to want to die.

Wild, wonderful West Virginia, it says on brochures. In the pictures, people raft down whitewater, hike through forests. Cows browse on green hills alongside untrafficked highways.

But driving through the valleys, it feels close, dark, the car twisting around curves. 35 M.P.H., the yellow signs warn. 20. 15. The farther from town, the fewer guardrails there are. Steep hills cut the sun, and roads narrow. Our stepfather drives his white Scout fast; our stomachs lean as we hug the sides of mountains. I rest my cheek against the glass, my book bag at my feet full of *Watchtowers* and *Awake!*s. We hurtle across creeks, not slowing for the narrow bridges. The gray-flecked asphalt flickers by. My eyes fall down the sides of hills, where dead leaves obscure old refrigerators, tires, farm equipment, splattered trash bags spilling diapers. The car goes fast through the dimness.

If I concentrate, I can almost feel the car going over the edge, feel it falling through the air like peace, see our crumpled bodies at the ravine bottom, and hear the silence, only leaves falling, until the consternation of rescue workers begins.

Suicide, I know, is a grave sin. If I do it, I will not be resurrected with the faithful to live forever on a Paradise earth. And wishing for something in your heart is the same as doing it, and Jehovah sees all and will punish.

Surreptitiously, as if Jehovah will not notice, I lean into the turns, adding my weight, relaxing my body against the metal and glass, longing for the wheels to stagger over the slight berm. *Now,* I think, but we keep going. Another yellow sign approaches. *Okay: now.* But we keep arriving at places unharmed.

Children are to be seen and not heard, my mother has said from the time we could toddle. *Hu-mil-i-ty,* she likes to say slowly, pronouncing it with a French accent for some reason, leaning over me, hand raised, teaching me not to have the prideful last word.

One evening at dinner my stepfather is talking, berating, dosing out punishments (my brother's Erector set, taken away for a year; his bicycle, chained under the trailer where he can see it, until he can perfect himself in God's sight), quoting scripture after scripture at our lowered faces. It is the fourth day we've had pancakes for dinner. There's nothing else to eat.

At the Kingdom Hall, we've been studying the letter to the Corinthians, the part about what love is. *Long-suffering and kind.* The phrase comes to me abruptly through the haze of his voice. *Kind.*

"You're a hypocrite," I say suddenly, laying my fork down on my plate. My brother stares at me. But it seems perfectly clear, suddenly. We've studied about the Pharisees and Sadducees, about those who pray out on the street corner instead of at home in their closets. Jehovah hates hypocrites. He will spit them out of his mouth. I look at my mother. It's the simple truth. Jehovah would want me to say it.

JOY CASTRO

"You're both hypocrites." I feel calm and dizzy, like I'm looking down on us all from far above.

There's a long moment of complete stillness, and then his fist plummets into my face. The ceiling blares. When I pull my chin down, they're all staring at me, and I lurch to my feet, almost happy. Everything seems perfectly clear — light, even — free. "It's true," I say, loud and giddy with it. My brother is staring wide-eyed, as though I've gone insane. I think, *Perhaps I have.* It feels cool and easy there. "You're hypocrites," I repeat. It feels too good to stop.

Our stepfather stands, too, and his knuckles spring toward my face again, and the knobby spindles of the room divider thud into my back. The rest of the night is blank.

He has always hated our reading, our books — even my mother's historical novels: James Michener, John Jakes. "Fairy tales," he says, in the same tone of disgust that he uses for *artistic.* He reads nothing but the Watchtower literature and the Bible, he says proudly again and again.

Finally, he takes our books away. They are worldly stories, written by worldly men and women. We must box them up. He takes them, sells them, keeps the money. My hutch stares emptily back at me.

We may read only Watchtower books and our schoolbooks for homework. We are not to bring any other books into the house. If we do, it will be the belt. Each evening, they check what we've brought home.

I am to throw away all my drawings, which are of worldly things: horses rearing, glamorous women lounging on ship rails, big Tudor mansions with pools. I may continue to draw, if I must, but I can only draw illustrations of Bible stories. This will keep my mind on godly subjects, not on the temptations of this world and its wicked system of things.

I draw a few biblical scenes from the different Kingdom Hall books, working on the draping of the clothes and the shading, and

124

then get sick of it. They're boring. I have to hold everything up for his inspection, have to make sure the pertinent scripture is lettered in the corner.

What I want to draw is a gigantic heel, mine, crushing the serpent's head, but he's not stupid. I stop drawing altogether.

My mother had long urged one of her favorite childhood books upon me, *The Secret Garden* by Frances Hodgson Burnett, a pale green paperback ringed with roses. I relished the part about the walled garden, dormant, storing its beauty until the children discover and care for it. The little locked door. But Mary is a girl I couldn't like, spoiled, pouting and sullen, openly angry. I prefer Burnett's *A Little Princess* and read it again and again.

The princess of the title, Sara Crewe, is not really royal. She is brought from India by her adoring father, a widower, to attend boarding school in London, where, due to his wealth, she is made the show pupil. Her dark curling hair and green eyes do not make her pretty as Lavinia is pretty, or like Isobel Grange, who had been the darling of the regiment. Nonetheless, there is something charming about Sara's serious, sweet face.

She's kind, as well. She tells stories to the scullery maid Becky, who falls asleep in front of Sara's fire, to orphaned Lottie, to fat Ermengarde, who can't pronounce French. Sara takes care of them and shares her luxuries.

But when her father dies, his diamond mines a failure, Miss Minchin banishes her to the attic, to a room next to Becky's. Sara discovers cold, hunger, and shame — and she learns them in front of the schoolgirls who once had envied her. Through it all, she makes up stories, weaving them aloud in the night to comfort Becky, describing a fire in the dark grate, and pink-iced cakes, and soft rugs on the frigid floors. She befriends a rat she names Melchisedec, gives her bread away to a starving street girl.

A Lascar from the house next door, lonely in England, listens through the little attic skylight and tells his employer about the strange little girl. Silently, secretly, he brings rich gifts in the night, all the things she describes. She wakes to find miracles, and keeps them hidden from Miss Minchin, sharing them with the girls who are her friends.

In the end, the Lascar's employer — her father's business partner, it turns out, who has moved to London to search for her and who has financed the Lascar's gifts — learns her true identity.

The mines have turned around; all has been a terrible mistake. Will she come live with him? And Becky, too? They do.

Miss Minchin is roundly chastised. The starving girl is taken in by a baker woman who has seen Sara's act of kindness in the street.

When my stepfather takes the book away, I know it already, can retell it to myself in clear detail. I lie in my cold bed at night and see again Captain Crewe disappearing in the horse-drawn cab, bound for the station, kissing and waving his hand as though his heart will break. When Sara takes his face in her hands, studying it, he asks if she is learning him by heart.

"No," she says solemnly. "I know you by heart. You are inside my heart."

I lie in the dark, concentrating, and a skylight silently opens in the trailer roof. I see the gentle eyes of the Lascar, bringing me hot food and tea.

One cold afternoon, walking the mile home from the bus stop, I feel the lining of my coat pocket give. It's an old, bulky coat, navy blue, waterproof and thickly lined, that had been my grandfather's. My mother took it when he died, when I was five or six. It's hung in various closets since, unused, a memento until now, when I've outgrown everything else and there's no money for new coats. My fingers squirm against the seam, pressing until more stitches snap. The hole widens enough for a book, a smallish paperback.

I smuggle books from the library onto the school bus and read them for the forty-five minutes of our ride. Then they get pushed deep into the lining of the coat, where my stepfather and mother never think to look.

Walking up the hill each morning, I feel the book's rectangle bump against my body like a perilous charm. I can read for another forty-five minutes on the bus. For an hour and a half each day, I evaporate into forbidden worlds: Tolkien's trilogy, its simple demarcations of good and evil coming as a welcome relief, and the names edible like poetry — Aragorn, Galadriel, the great horse Shadowfax. I read a whole library shelf's worth of Helen MacInnes's Cold War espionage novels, in which Cambridge dons and their pretty wives stumble into intrigue abroad, wittily eluding disaster. I want to be the don. I want to be the pretty wife. I long to walk down avenues lined with trees in blossom and slip beneath a gothic arch into the lecture hall.

The hole widens farther. I take larger books. I never finish one crucial 1950s hardback, its blue binding worn to white at the corners. It features a girl who goes to college, something Witnesses do not do, something no one in our family has done.

College, as forbidden as sex. It's so delicious, that world of sweater sets and knowledge, that I take the book out to read late at night and hide it under clothes in my drawer. My mother finds it. She won't tell him, she says, but I've got to take it back immediately. I don't even care. I return it, lighthearted. I've begun to plot a private future.

Many years later, preparing to teach for the first time *Heart of Darkness,* a book I'd never liked, I read biographies of Conrad and feel a sudden sympathy. Exiled, orphaned, kept by an uncle who recorded in a ledger every expense incurred by his upbringing, he ran away to sea at seventeen. But through it all, he read: Shakespeare, Dickens, Dostoevsky.

"I do not know what would have become of me," he wrote, "had I not been a reading boy."

*　　*　　*

"You got some fat on those thighs," my stepfather says. "Fat thighs, you don't want. Trust me. How you gonna get a husband?"

I am in bed, my nightgown pulled up to my hips. There is no fat. I am gaunt, like a dancer, but without a dancer's grace. My thighs knock into desks at school, startling me. I move carefully now. If I go too fast, I walk into tables, doorways, walls, bruise my legs, make a fool of myself, as though I have no sense of where my body leaves off and the space around me begins.

I am hungry all the time now. After I eat my free lunch in the cafeteria, I go up to the snack bar and stare down the boy behind the counter. I order chocolate ice cream bars and when he says, "Fifty cents," I just look at him and pull the wrapper off. I take a bite, staring at him until he turns away.

But still my stomach falls like a deep bowl between my hip-bones when I lie on my back, and my hands tremble. All the time, I am tired.

My stepfather takes my thighs in his hands and begins to squeeze them, pull them. "Massage them like this, take the fat right off," he says. Up and down his hands move, squeezing hard. His thumbs graze across the crotch of my underwear, but he says nothing and his face doesn't change, as if he hasn't noticed.

Again, they graze. Then the sides of his hands chop against my crotch.

I stare up at the ceiling, its small white swirls of plaster, like the waves of an ocean, and underneath, just beyond where I can see them, there could be mermaids swimming, and seaweed fronds billowing in the current, and there's a castle encrusted with pearls, and mermen wear gold crowns in their wavy hair.

Then he jerks my gown down over my knees and leaves.

Each night he comes into my room, into my bed. To say good night. To massage me, which my mother says will do me good. His large hands clamp my shoulders. "Got some tension there," he says.

He pushes my nightgown aside, down onto the tops of my arms. "Get a better grip," he says.

Complaining, moving, pulling away have not worked. Even crying.

"Shh," he says when I cry. He likes it. "Is my baby girl upset? Let me make it better." And the rubbing just lasts longer.

When I tell her I am nervous and where the hands go, my mother says, "Oh, please. Stop exaggerating. He probably wasn't even aware of it. He's just trying to get to know you." She looks at me sternly. "He really wants you to like him, you know."

Now I just lie still, unmoving, unspeaking. Sometimes he lies next to me on top of the bedspread, lies on his stomach in his T-shirt and underwear, his breath growing heavier and quicker in the dark. Abruptly, he will rise and go.

When supper ends each evening, my brother is ordered to his room, and our mother and stepfather disappear down the hallway to theirs. I clear the table, run the dishwater, and take my place at the sink under the single bulb. If he hears the refrigerator or any cabinets opening, I'll get the belt.

In winter, the world outside the window is already black, and my own face is reflected back as I wash. I study myself. I have large eyes, a wide, soft mouth that glows pink even in the black glass, cheeks hollow now like a model's in a magazine, smooth dark hair. There's something steady about my jaw.

Our stepfather buys bags of walnuts from which no one else is allowed to eat. I crave nuts, meat, beans, milk — anything with protein. Sometimes when he wanders the house, munching, with the bag cradled open in his hand, I feel the back of my neck shake with heat, and I imagine killing him for them.

The benefit of his great height and heaviness is that we can hear him approach; the trailer, perched on cement blocks, quakes with his every step. The hallway between their bedroom and the kitchen takes four strides; I have plenty of warning, should he decide to emerge.

When it is quiet, only the sound of water swishing, I ease open the door of the high cupboard to my left, stirring the dishes with my right hand so they continue clinking peacefully against each other. Without looking, I feel for the bag until its lumpy cellophane bulge rests under my hand. With fingers and thumb, I twist the metal tie and spread open the neck. Two, or three, at most, or he'll notice. Into my mouth immediately. Then the closing of the bag, the twisting of the tie, and the silent easing shut of the cupboard door.

I close my eyes and chew, just standing there, the buttery squeeze of them in my teeth, my right hand still circling in the sink.

At night I break the rules to go into my brother's room. He's huddled on the linoleum, his ear pressed to the heat vent. I curl down to listen and put my arm around his back.

At the far end of the trailer, our stepfather's beating her.

"Who's the head of this household?" he yells.

She sobs indistinguishable things.

"Then are you going to respect me? Are you gonna show me some respect?" We hear something big slamming into something else, a wall, a dresser.

She screams.

"You're like the stiff-necked people of Israel, who would not obey Jehovah," he yells. She screams, there are thuds, he yells scriptures at her, it goes on forever. I keep my arm tight around my brother. We both stare into the metal slits.

"It's okay," I whisper in the lulls. "It'll be okay." Tony cries with his mouth shut, and I push the tears from his cheeks with my fingers. "It's okay," I repeat, until the noises stop. "There, you see?" He gives me a sudden terrified look, vaults into his bed, pulls the covers up, and feigns instant sleep. He's felt what I haven't: the vibrations of our stepfather's footfalls.

I slip into my room. The steps cross the living room and move into our hall. He pauses at Tony's door, wheezing.

Anything could set him off. He's torn him from sleep before, beaten him in his pajamas for a weed left unscythed.

I call his name.

"What do you want?" he growls.

"Is everything okay? I thought I heard something."

He stands there in Tony's doorway for a long minute.

I add, "I can't sleep."

He clears his throat. The wet phlegm rattles. "A little massage will relax you," he says finally, and he comes into my room.

11

It's the summer after my freshman year in high school. I am thirteen. There is not enough to keep us busy, our stepfather says: not enough brush to cut, not enough ditches to dig, not enough cement to chip off secondhand concrete blocks with a chisel and hammer until my hands bleed.

Tony, eight, crouches with a sickle during the long evenings, barely visible from the trailer, until my stepfather calls him in. I mow the acres of bottomland from the creek to the dirt road.

The trailer has no gas hookup. A ditch needs to be dug from a gas well on a hill. Three feet deep. I go out after breakfast each day alone with the shovel, and my stepfather comes out periodically to check on my progress.

My English teacher has given me an old pink paperback, *The Brothers Karamazov*. "I'd like you to try this," he'd said quietly at the end of the semester, putting it into my hands, nodding at me with his serious look. I hide the book in different places in my room and then smuggle it out to the ditch in the loosening waistband of my jeans. It is my first exposure to the shell-shocked sensibilities of Dostoevsky, whose characters struggle to understand how a good God can allow cruelty to innocents.

I dig fast to make progress, and when I cannot lift another shov-
elful, I stand there and read Dostoevsky, ready to shove it back in my
jeans if my stepfather comes around the bend to check on me. Then
I dig, and the story keeps going in my head. I read and correct where
I've gone wrong. I read the whole book that way.

I don't know why we go to the swimming pool. We don't go anywhere else: no movies, no parks, no baseball games. And the swimming pool costs money, which he always says we don't have. But
several times each summer, we go.

The cool water feels good, and it's sweet to see my brother
briefly happy, splashing in the shallow end with other children, but I
hate it. It's embarrassing. The pool is right next to the high school; I
see people I know. My swimsuit is two years old, a little girl's suit,
and tight everywhere.

I'm standing by the fence, high chain-link so people can't climb
over, when the boy I like, the worldly boy I write in my diary about,
Tommy Singleton, a football player a year ahead of me, comes up to
talk. Tommy Singleton, talking to me. The handsomest boy in the
sophomore class. I can't think. I hook my index fingers in the back of
my bottoms and pull them down over my butt more.

A sudden weight falls across my shoulders. My stepfather's
thick arm.

"You talking to my little girl, are you?" He leans against the
chain-link, and it bellies outward with his bulk. His great gut is matted black with hair above his shorts. "She a nice girl, do you think?"

The long length of his skin is pressed hot against my side. The
stink of his sweat is all I can smell. My throat thickens.

"I'm going to get a drink of water," I say, slipping out, and Tommy
doesn't talk to me again.

Our stepfather drives us in the *FARM USE* truck up a rutted moun-
tainside to gather firewood as he cuts it. Our mother stays down at

the trailer, baking. The chainsaw buzzes, we pick up the pieces that fall, run to the truckbed, stack them, and run back.

"You keep your hands out of the way, you hear?" he says. "'Cause I'm not stopping this thing. You wanna lose a finger, boy?" he roars. Tony shakes his head, eyes lowered. "Then you keep moving. You watch that blade. 'Cause I don't give a shit where your hands are." It is a grim parody of Brother Cairns and Shelley, their silent accord.

When we do not move fast enough — when our hands are not there to catch the falling chunk — he hits us. When my brother, arms full of wood, does not run fast enough to the truck, he kicks him in the thigh. The toes of his boots are steel, I know; I have to clean them. Tony staggers and keeps running.

We return to the trailer, muddy and bruised, and stack the truckload of wood outside while he goes in. When we enter, he's showered, watching television and eating fresh apple pie with our mother. We go silently to our rooms and wait for permission to bathe.

But all these things are not enough to keep us busy, he says, and idle hands are asking for Satan. We will auxiliary pioneer. Together, as a family. We will take a territory where there is no Kingdom Hall, and we will go as missionaries proclaiming the good news of God's kingdom. Full-time pioneers go door-to-door one hundred hours a month. "And there's no reason we can't do that, eventually. Can't we, Mother?" our stepfather says, since neither of them works. But we will begin slowly, auxiliary pioneering sixty hours a month.

Wyoming County lies toward the southern edge of West Virginia, remote from even towns like Bluefield and Beckley. Its villages are called Wolf Pen, Jesse, Bud. But Tony and I are not shown the map. We don't know where we're going. We know only what we can glean from what they say in front of us. This is going to be the real Appalachia, our stepfather says. We think we have it hard? These people are the real McCoy.

Silent, obedient, we pack overnight bags and stuff our book bags full of *Watchtower*s, *Awake!*s, and truth books. Do we have enough service slips, the little forms for recording back-calls, new subscriptions, and Bible studies, for marking down the number of hours out in service, to be slid through the slit in the wooden box and tallied at Bethel in Brooklyn each year? We get more at the Kingdom Hall.

Our stepfather drives; they argue on the road about directions, fuel, money. He orders me to rub my mother's shoulders. She's getting out of hand, he says. She needs to calm down, or there's going to be trouble when we stop. I lean forward and rub.

"You don't stop till I say you stop," he says. She sits there, mute and unresponsive under my hands. We arrive.

The land is green and rolling and remote. From up on the ridges, we can see smooth forested hills for miles. Tarpaper shacks perch on the edges of hillsides, with dogs growling under the porch as we approach. The houses are so far apart we cannot walk from one to another, as we do in neighborhoods, so we drive between them on the soft dirt roads, taking turns which pair gets out: Tony goes with our mother; our stepfather takes me. Two by two we go, like animals emerging from the ark. White-painted tires, turned inside out, sit in the yards, their edges cut in zigzags, full of flowers or staked tomatoes.

Some houses have no running water. Some have no electricity. Some quiver at the top of ridges, only two thin tire paths down to the road, mountains all around. Garbage spills between trees down the sides of ravines. At some houses, packs of thin dogs circle the car, growling and barking, until a man in overalls emerges from behind a barn. At others, women come to their doors in flowered dresses and invite us in to sit on their sofas. They are plump, with soft arm flesh that waves when they gesture. Their mouths keep collapsing inward as they speak. Some people refuse the books because they can't read, others because they don't have a quarter. We give tracts away for free and promise to return and discuss them. When we quote scriptures, sometimes they quote back at us. People don't yell or slam the door like they do in towns. They're happy to sit a spell.

My stepfather swings his heavy book bag as we walk to the doors. His pants are brown polyester, and he wears an undershirt beneath his short-sleeved white shirt. Each day he wears the same mud-green tie. In the heat, his bare scalp sweats, and the gray hair around its edges dampens to black strands. He coughs and spits into a handkerchief, which he stuffs back in his pocket.

At the door, he pulls out his Bible with quick, powerful motions, opening quickly to the right scripture, talking loudly over them when they interrupt, smiling his oily smile. I stand in my place beside him — sometimes he grabs my arm and pulls me closer before the door opens — and look down, edging my eyes around the porch or room to see what's there.

When it's my turn, I yawn, nervous, knowing he will berate me for any missed opportunity, any relevant scripture I fail to use. The women look kindly into my eyes, nodding, smiling, but unless I place something, there will be trouble.

On our first trip, we stay in a motel. It is expensive, but it's for Jehovah. The flat turquoise carpet peels up along the walls. My mother has brought along the plug-in saucepan and boxes of Beefaroni, which she prepares in the corner on the floor. He says the blessing, and we eat on paper plates, sitting on the floor. He goes over our mistakes of the day and beats my brother.

I sleep on the other double bed, and Tony sleeps on the floor. No sleeping in the same bed, no perversions.

We get up and do it again. For lunch, he pulls off the road. My mother opens the cooler and passes out food: two peanut butter sandwiches for him, one for her, half for me, and one-quarter of a sandwich, loose inside its clear plastic bag, for my brother.

Are there four trips down to Wyoming County? Seven? They blur. I begin to recognize landmarks on every road we take.

He brooks no disagreement now, not even from my mother. Beating quiets her only for a while, so he has a new approach. "You want to argue?" he says, pushing his face into her face, daring her to speak. "You got anything to say?"

If she replies, he beats Tony. She and I have to watch. This mostly works, and she stops arguing. Anything he says, we do. We watch him and guess what he's going to say before he says it. We do it before he opens his mouth.

But there is no escape. When we learn to follow a rule, he makes it harder. When we learn that, he changes it. When my brother's nails are dirty after working outside, he is beaten for filthiness. If he trips, he is beaten for clumsiness.

"You looking me in the eye, boy?" our stepfather roars, shoving himself back from the table, Tony whispering, "No, sir," into his plate. "What's that? You talking back to me? You saying I'm a liar?" He yanks him from the chair and beats him in front of us, yelling, "Don't you stop eating" at my mother and me, the long leather strap snapping against itself in the air when he draws back, my brother's body jerking, my spoon mechanically lowering and rising, the food thickening in my throat like paste.

Our last trip down to Wyoming County is special. We stay at Twin Falls Resort State Park, in the lodge. Each time we've passed the sign, he's said we can't afford it. Now we're there, staying in a pretty room with sliding glass doors and a terrace. We eat in the restaurant, where there are tablecloths. The front-desk people give us extra sheets to make up a bed on the floor for my brother. My stepfather gets more and more tense.

At night, my mother is crying in bed. He is muttering something at her. I reach across the dark span of floor to take her hand, and she grabs on and squeezes.

"No," she whispers. "They're still awake." He grunts angrily. Tony is asleep; I can hear his sleep-breathing. "No," my mother whispers again, louder, with a sob. I hear the thud of his flesh hitting her flesh, and her hand spasms in mine. Her fingernails dig. Then she lets go. I hear them muttering and moving, and then the glass doors slide open and shut, and there is nearly silence, only broken by a grunt now and then. I lie there staring into the dark space of the room. Something ruptures silently in my head. They do not come back while I am awake.

In the morning, my brother is still sleeping on the floor when our stepfather is ready to cross to the bathroom.

"Get up, dummy!" he yells, kicking him in the head. My brother cries out once, clutching the sheet to his head and lurching into the corner. "Don't you pay no attention to him," he yells at my mother, closing the door. She stays in the bed, compliant, until he comes out and can watch that all she's doing is dressing. Tony sobs silently as he puts on his clothes.

Dressed for service, we go directly to the restaurant, where our stepfather stares at my breasts across the table. His knee keeps rubbing against my knee. Around us, families are eating, dressed in jeans and T-shirts for hiking. They are laughing. A mother is leaning over to brush her son's cheek. There's a sense of ease and pleasure, of comfort and enough of everything. But something about the place makes him angrier than ever.

"That's it, boy," he says, when my brother spills his orange juice on the white cloth. It's what he says when there will be a beating. It's a triumphant, final sound: "That's it." My brother's face crumples. "Don't you cry, boy," he says in a lower tone. "Don't you cry, or you'll get double."

"You get in the car," he says to our mother and me, after the check is paid. He hauls Tony by the arm toward the hotel room. We put our book bags in the Scout but cannot get in. We stand by the open doors, facing each other across the roof. I look at my mother's face, dead and blank, but she won't look at me; she stares past into the trees. We say nothing. They are gone ten minutes, twenty, they are never coming back; my brother is dead, I think, in the pretty room with the sliding doors. Inside the restaurant, I can see people still eating, smiling. All around the lodge, the branches of evergreens swing in long dark curves.

And then they appear, our stepfather filling the door, my brother behind. They cross the road to us. Tony limps. My mother does not turn around to see. His eyes are like punched holes as he meets mine; his mouth is open in an *O*, the breath whistling in and out. A red hand-shaped welt is swelling on his cheek. His face is dry.

"You better not let me see you cry, boy," our stepfather says, getting into the driver's side, the keys already in his hand.

My brother doesn't cry. He eases into the backseat and pulls the seatbelt around himself. For a moment the metal shakes and will not go in. And then it goes in. We look at each other. Then the car starts, and he looks at his lap. No one says anything on the drive north.

"The body," I read somewhere once, "is the toy they cannot take away." I thought it was a clever thing to write.

But they can take it away. The person who wrote that didn't know.

School starts again, and with it comes the end of pioneering and the relief of early darkness, of having to do homework, a lightening of the chores. Doing dishes, I palm a steak knife from the kitchen, easing the drawer silently open, sliding it into my pocket. In bed, I slip it under the other pillow, practice grabbing it in the dark, my hand darting fast as a rabbit's dash to catch its handle.

He finds it, lying beside me in the darkness as he has begun to do, breathing, his whole body stiff and heavy next to me in the bed. First, on top of the bedspread. Now between the sheets.

I think of nothing. I do not pray. I lie there in a stillness so extreme I might be dead, each nerve a wire humming with still terror.

"And what's this?" he says. He sits up. "Turn that light on." I do. The room jumps to brightness, and I pull my arm back to my side. Only my eyes swerve to see the knife gripped in his hand.

"What you got this for, girly?"

I look at the window, the door, long for my mother to appear. "It's so isolated here. I get afraid. Of robbers, I mean." My voice is strangled, unbelievable.

"Is that so?" His grin leaks slowly across his mouth. It's a good game, cat and mouse. "Robbers."

"Yes. It's isolated here," I say.

"Well, no robbers are gonna get you. I'm here. I'm here to protect my little girl. You don't need this." He rises and moves around the bed to stand above me. "We don't want you cutting yourself by accident, do we? A sharp knife like this?" He holds the blade in my face. I push my head backward into the pillow.

"No, sir," I whisper.

"Then I'll just take this back to the kitchen." Quick as a fox, his free hand reaches out and flips back the blankets, unzips my quilted pink nightgown, sternum to crotch, flips the fabric open. He stares down at me, my breasts, my hipbones, my white underwear. His eyes glitter. He grins down for a minute.

"So cover yourself up," he says. My hands fly to my waist, but the zipper snags, sticks, jerks upward. "Don't be so modest," he laughs. "Fathers have a right to see their daughters. It's natural." The corners of the room are thick with shadow. "And what am I?"

"My spiritual father," I whisper. I am a wax doll, empty, pliant, a cunning image of the girl who used to live here.

"That's right." The lamp clicks. The darkness becomes deeper darkness. "No more knives. You hear?"

"Yes, sir."

His steps shake the trailer as he moves down the hall.

He decides to begin a photography business: a new start, more money. My mother will do the books and paperwork, and he will take the pictures. They leave us alone on Saturdays with unfinishable lists of chores while they shoot Witness weddings in other towns.

They put ads in local newspapers: *MODELS WANTED — For*

commercials, any age, from babies to grandparents. No experience necessary.

There aren't really going to be any commercials; that's to lure people in. But there are big companies in New York, photo banks, that buy all kinds of pictures for advertisers to use, and they pay good money. My stepfather has sold things to them before. If a model in one of his photographs gets spotted in New York, it could lead to a commercial. So it's not technically a lie.

Apply in person only. And then the date and the room number of the cheap motel where they'll rent two rooms, one for my mother to do intake, where the people sign release forms and wait their turn, and the other for my stepfather to take the pictures in.

This could be your big chance. Don't miss it.

He's gone for the day; we don't know where. When our mother asks me to put away laundry in their room, a territory we never enter, I am surprised, but I don't ask questions anymore. I carry the folded stacks, still warm, from the dryer to her dresser, looking quickly around at everything in this room I never see. A mirror. The bed. A punched indentation in the wall.

I can remember the pattern of my mother's drawers from before; I know where the underwear will go, the bras, the shirts. She's in the kitchen, humming a song from the songbook. I open another drawer, looking for a place to put pants.

Inside lies a box. On the box is pictured a long white object with a cord; I know instantly what it must be. Even the cursive is sexy, with extra curls flowing into the corners.

Next to the box is an envelope. The envelope says *MOM* in his chaotic capitals. She's still humming down the hall. I slide the card out and open it. *WANNA FUCK?* his printing asks. I put it back and shove the stack of pants in the drawer.

That night, I write in my diary, trying to work out the shock of it. She had cried when he beat us. He had slammed her body against the wall, hit her till she bled, spat in her face. I had believed she was miserable, captive, like we were. The box and its strange white appliance glimmer in front of my eyes. I don't know what to do with this, this evidence of some kind of pleasure, mutuality. Playfulness, even. My mother never says the word *fuck.* My mother does not approve of slang — we are not even supposed to say *wanna* or *shut up* or *no way,* much less cursing. My hand shakes as I write it all down in the small blue book, after the entry about which boys smile at me in the halls.

A week later, coming in to tell me good night, she sits on the edge of my bed. Her arms are crossed, her face puffed with an anger she never shows when our stepfather can see.

"You are never to go into my room again," she hisses. "Do you understand me?"

"Okay." I examine a strand of my hair for split ends.

"I know what you did." I don't look at her. "I know what you got into in my room, young lady." I say nothing. "I *know.* I read it in your diary." I gasp and look up into her pinched face.

"You read my diary?" All the secrets I've written careen through my head: all the worldly boys whose forbidden charms I've listed, and how Shari, the majorette with kind eyes who sometimes smiles at me, and I will have an apartment in Water Tower Place, wearing matching cardigans and riding the glass elevators and the long twin escalators with the potted vines and water falling down the polished brown granite between them. I think of how I'd written down word-for-word the arguments my brother and I had heard, crouched together illicitly over the vent.

"What's in my room is none of your business, do you hear?" Everything she says is a hot whisper close to my face. Her mouth smells stale, like the breath of someone old. "Do you understand me?"

"Yes," I say, vowing, *I will never write in my diary again.*

Her voice grows louder, normal, even pleasant, the fake-pleasant that's her usual tone. My stepfather is in the living room, watching television, and she points her face that way, but her eyes stay on me. "You can come tell her good night now." She walks down the hall. He clears his throat and spits in his handkerchief as he rises.

When I'm nineteen and in college, my mother and I enjoy one of our brief détentes.

She only married my stepfather, she tells me on the phone, because he threatened to expose her. She'd had sex with him before they married — he pushed her to, she says, there on our old plaid couch in the family room — and he threatened to tell the elders. She would have been publicly reproved for fornication in front of the congregation. So she married him instead.

I'm stunned. I can hardly hold the information she's telling me.

"So you didn't want to marry him? Not even at the wedding?"

"No, of course not. Not at all." I'm uncertain, thinking of the promised income, the card and vibrator in her drawer, and wondering what the truth is. But it's too embarrassing to discuss, and I don't want to wreck her sudden candor.

"But he would have been reproved, too," I say.

"He said it wouldn't bother him. He said if I didn't marry him, he would tell."

"Well, okay, but so what? Ten minutes of embarrassment. Bam, it's over."

"Humiliated like that? In front of my brothers and sisters?" she says, incredulous. "Never."

"Well, but if Jehovah's the one you were worried about sinning against, didn't he already know anyway?"

"That's different." Her voice closes in irritation.

"So you stuck with him for two years? Because you didn't want to be embarrassed?" I feel like throwing up. I've put a thousand miles between myself and that world; the whole thing sounds bizarrely outré, *Scarlet Letter*ish to me. "Wouldn't it have been better to just get it over with? Take the reproof and move on?"

"I couldn't," she says. "I just couldn't."

*　　*　　*

A new family moves into town, to the Kingdom Hall. Our mother had known them from before, years ago, at our Bridgeport congregation. There's a little boy, my brother's age. The husband, with a daughter a little older than I am, is an elder. After discussion, my stepfather agrees that my brother and I can go there for an afternoon, on our own, as a kind of trial, to see if we can behave ourselves. It is the first time in over a year we have been at someone's house without his monitoring.

I've liked Tessa since the first time I'd seen her at the Kingdom Hall. She has blond curls and merry blue eyes. Her cheeks curve; she's almost plump, but not quite. Solid.

As soon as we are in her room, we sit cross-legged on her bed and I tell her everything: the beatings, the food rules, the yelling — everything except the weird white appliance and the touching at night, for which I have no words and about which I do not think. She is shocked and sincere. We go to her parents and tell them. Her father says this will be taken care of. It is not Jehovah's way. He will talk to the elders, and they will have a talk with my stepfather. It will be taken care of.

When we arrive back home, the interrogation begins, as it always had when we came back from my father's. Like then, I tell the truth: yes, I've told them about everything that happens here. Yes, they say Jehovah would not approve of such treatment of women and children, and Sister Desmond is very upset about what you're doing to Mom, and Brother Desmond is going to have a discussion with the other elders.

We are at the trailer for only ten minutes before he tells me to get back into the Scout. He drives me to their house alone.

When we arrive, he grabs my shoulder and steers me up to their porch. His voice is loud, but the words he says are polite. He would like to speak to Tessa and the father. They come out on the porch. The day is warm, lazy, sunny. The mown lawn slopes away from the house down the hill.

"We've got a little problem on our hands here," he says. He tells me to confess to them that I have lied.

"I wasn't lying."

He orders me again. Concern grows on Brother Desmond's face, and Tessa looks angry and scared.

"She's a liar," my stepfather says. "She lies all the time. We don't know what we're going to do with her."

"I'm not lying. I'm not going to say I lied, because I didn't." I look into Brother Desmond's eyes. "Everything I said was the truth." I know I'm going to get the belt. Bad.

"You hear how rebellious she is?"

We go back and forth. My shoulder goes numb in his grip. Brother Desmond looks more and more agitated, and his wife comes out. He's an older man, with gray hair. They link their arms together.

I turn toward my stepfather, my voice even. "When I got home, I didn't lie to you about what I told them, even though I knew you'd beat me. Why would I lie to them now?" I love watching the flesh around his eyes shrink tight when I speak; I know he won't hit me in front of them. We go around and around, while the Desmonds stare. "Why would I lie? Jehovah hates a liar," I say. "Which means he can't be all that fond of you right now." His face flashes like he's going to slap me, but he doesn't. Finally, his demand shifts.

"Then you better say that, whether you're lying or not lying, it is not your *place* to go repeating what happens in the privacy of our home. I am the head of the household. I tell people what happens and doesn't happen."

I look at him, incredulous. It's as good as an admission.

"It's not my place to tell the truth?" I speak slowly. I feel like I'm in a stage play with an idiot. "If I say that, we can go?"

"Tell them."

I look into their faces, one by one. Tessa is crying. "Whether I'm lying or not lying," I repeat carefully, "it is not my place to tell the truth about what goes on in our house."

"But she is lying," he says quickly. "She's a liar. And what happens in our house is none of your business." His voice gets meaner, and he leans toward the man. He points his index finger at the man's chest, the way he used to thump it into my father's chest, but doesn't touch him. "You got that?"

They nod. We leave.

At the Kingdom Hall, we see them three times a week, and they don't look at me or my stepfather. Sister Desmond always stops to chat with my mother, always strokes my brother's hair. But nothing happens, except that my brother and I don't go to anyone's house alone again.

In Book II of the *Republic,* Socrates warns Adeimantus about the kinds of stories that poets must not tell. He gives examples, stories of the gods. In each, a parent abuses a child, or a husband his wife. In a few, a child rises up in fury and enacts vengeance.

These are the kinds of stories, Plato argues, that *must not be admitted into our state* but must instead *be buried in silence.* They undermine the rule of family, and thus the rule of government. Worse yet, the stories' offenders are gods, the gods of Greek myth: church, state, and family collapse at the telling of a tale.

Once I was taken alone to a house in the country. Strange elders filled it. A sister was there to cook the meals. They spent the weekend convincing me to accept my place, to accept Jehovah's will. I was making things difficult. They took me on long, patient walks down leafy roads, trying to make me see.

Before we moved away to the trailer, I asked for an audience with the circuit overseer, who went from Kingdom Hall to Kingdom Hall, an elder among elders. He sat at one end of a long table in a closed room, and I sat at the other. Elders sat on both sides, like a tribunal. I described our stepfather's new rule. We had been eating and talking with our father for years, I said, and still we were good

Witnesses. Our stepfather hit us, cursed at us, and said he didn't want us, which our father, disfellowshipped, didn't do.

Our stepfather's interpretations of scripture were unusual, I was told, but not unheard of. It was, perhaps, not the most compassionate way of dealing with a disfellowshipped person. But he was the head of our household now. He had been at Bethel. There had been no other complaints about him. I was a child and a girl. My role was to submit.

As a high school freshman and sophomore, I daydream through history class, through all discussions of politics, secure in the belief that Jehovah will wipe out the governments of this world, and the wicked system of things will be no more, but will be replaced by his Paradise kingdom in the twinkling of an eye. The nations of Christendom are the wild beast in Revelation, and the United Nations is the whore of Babylon, who rides the wild beast's back. The mark of the beast might be those little stripes that are being put on all the groceries now; we're not sure. At home, we read the dusky blue book *Our Incoming World Government — God's Kingdom,* about the glorious Bible prophecies of Jehovah's rulership. All our needs and desires will be satisfied. Armageddon will be coming along any day. When the teachers lecture, I whistle in my mind.

But some things catch even my attention. When my stepfather is out of earshot, I take to calling my mother Josef. "Thank you, Josef," I say politely. She looks at me, puzzled. I know she is thinking of the biblical Joseph, the one with the coat of many colors who sucks up to Pharaoh and knows what dreams mean. "Yes, Josef," I say when she tells me to do something. I know she won't tell him; she can't stand to be the cause of our beatings.

It gets boring, so I start saying it with more of what I think is a Russian accent. She guesses finally, her lips a flattened slit, and I give it up.

Now, as an adult, I cannot remember many such moments of rebellion. When I think back on those years, I remember our mute, immediate obedience and the crushing shroud of fear. I remember telling the truth despite terror, because I believed it was right, but not rebelling for rebellion's sake. Yet Tony swears that on Sundays, after the meeting but before going out in service, our stepfather would drive to Hardee's. We would go through the drive-through and take our meals back to the Kingdom Hall, eating them in the parking lot until the other brothers and sisters arrived from lunch at a restaurant or at home and we would organize into pairs and be assigned to our territories.

Idling in front of the Hardee's menu marquee, he would ask us what we wanted. We knew it was a test: we were supposed to request the smallest, cheapest roast beef sandwich on the menu, the one that cost a dollar, and no french fries or drink. This was to show our humility and our understanding of the fact that we didn't have a lot of money. Our stepfather would order large sandwiches and fries and sometimes a hot turnover. This was because he was a large man and the head of the household.

According to my brother, when my stepfather would ask, "Okay, what do you want?" I would reply, "Roast duck a l'orange." It was something my father brought home from the airplanes when we lived in England: leftover first-class meals for my mother to heat up at home, food with French names, still covered with crimped foil. The duck, sweet and sour like Chinese food, was my favorite as a five-year-old.

Our stepfather would twist around in the seat to glare at me.

"Well, you asked what we *wanted,* and that's what I actually want," I would say. I have no recollection of this, or of its consequences. It seems flagrant, hilarious, kamikaze-like, a crazed thing to say, but it makes me happy, and it makes me happy to know my brother remembers it, and that it makes us laugh, there on the sheltered porch of my house in Texas when he comes down to stand in my wedding and stays for good, and that it gave him courage then.

I have no language for the things my stepfather does; I cannot be sure if they are wrong or not. Only rape is clear to me, a word I've heard before, and there is no raping, no penis in vagina. I know no words for the frightening way I can't breathe when the hands brush against my crotch or the sides of my breasts, the tops of them, the bottoms of them, the way he pushes down my gown or inches my shirt off my shoulders, the way he stares at my body, talks about my *ass*, my *titties*, words that Witnesses don't use. The way I lie there stiff and silent, thinking, *Perhaps he does not notice, perhaps he does not realize.*

But rape they've talked about in the Kingdom Hall; it's in the Bible. And I know from health class what it is.

One day, while he's away somewhere, I go to my mother in the hallway of the trailer.

"I'm scared," I stammer. I'm scared to say it to her, too: scared of her anger, of her rejection, of her constant claims that I'm exaggerating, which make me wonder if I am, if I'm imagining things like she says I am. But I have to tell her. Each night, it's something new, some further push. "I'm scared he's going to rape me."

"Don't be ridiculous," she says. Her face is weary and irritated. "You're just being melodramatic."

"No, really," I say. "The way he touches me, it's getting worse. And he lays there in the bed, and he looks at me so weird—"

"You just stop it," she breaks in. "Just stop it right now." She's lost her patience. "That's enough with your disgusting lies." She looks around, as if to make sure my brother is nowhere nearby. She leans up into my face. "Don't you ever let me hear you mention this again, do you understand?"

I'm crying and cannot speak.

"Do you understand, young lady?"

I nod.

"Ridiculous," she says, turning away down the hall. "What would any man see in you?"

The way to make my stepfather a pie is this. First, you make the crust, the light, flaking, curling crust he requires every day. My mother does this with her family recipe and sets it aside. I meet her at the wooden table in the yard, each of us holding a small knife.

Then you peel the apples — the small, sweet ones, the kind he likes. You cut them in half, top to bottom, straight through the center. You cut the halves in half, scoop the core out with the knife, following the lines in the apple's pale meat, and slice the cored quarters. The slices will go into the crust, the dish into the oven, two pieces, hot, will be served in their bowls, and his will get a scoop of Breyers vanilla ice cream. Many times he tells us it's the best ice cream, as BMW is the best motorbike and Nikon is the best camera. Both of which he has. "Bavarian Motor Works," he likes to bellow, apropos of nothing.

I do not eat pie. It is a punishment. "Five desserts!" our stepfather yells when I err, leaping triumphantly to his feet to make the little marks, *HH*, on the kitchen chalkboard. When I run away, I am up to seventy-six desserts. I never reach zero. When I am close, he's more watchful. He loves to let me get to two or three.

It's fall. He's inside watching television. My mother and I sit in the yard, peeling, coring, slicing. The glossy apples disappear under our knives, emerge as neat pale slivers lying flat in the dish. I feel the slight resistance of the flesh, then the final quick thunk as the blade hits board.

"I don't know what I'm going to do," she says in a low smothered voice.

I carve a red curling spiral away from the flesh. She glances at me, sighs noisily. "I just don't know what I'm going to do."

"What about?"

"About him."

I think she's going to talk about running again. I'm sick of running, sick of waking in the motel bed halfway through Ohio only to hear her whispering into the phone, promising, apologizing, giving him directions. I'm sick of the pains in my stomach when we head back east again. Maybe she's starting to plan, I think. But we have no second car to run in now. He sold it after the last time. There's no money for Greyhound tickets. We're twelve miles outside a little town in rural West Virginia. We know no one but Witnesses.

And we've been through that, spent nights at elders' houses, the blood drying on her lip, her eye blacked, Tony bruised and shaking, the two of us huddled silent on a strange couch. They would like to help. They would. But they send us home. It's a family situation, a private matter. They acknowledge the rule my stepfather holds over her like a swinging blade: Except in cases of adultery, a wife cannot divorce her husband. It's a sin. We go back.

But leaving isn't on her mind.

"I don't know what it's going to take." My quarters fall into clean fans of slices, which I gather and drop in the dish.

"What what's going to take?"

"What it's going to take to satisfy him."

My knife steadies itself against the board. "Meaning what?"

"He's never satisfied." Her voice drops to a whisper. "Nothing I do." She pushes a long lock of gray back from her face. All the curl's fallen out of it. "Three, four times a day he wants it."

I cut my last apple through its center.

"You're a big girl. You know what I mean."

The halves into halves. The half-moons of the cores, the pith and seeds into the pot of waste.

"I could lose my mind," she says, her voice breaking. I stop cutting and look up. She's crying, but her hands don't stop moving. I can hear the creek. Tony is scything dead weeds in the distance. "I think it might kill me or something." She keeps her eyes on her apple, her knife. The trees rise dark up the mountain behind her. "He needs some other kind of — some kind of outlet." The only sound is her knife hitting the board as the slices separate.

I stare at her, at the wide dark bowl of the valley we live in. She glances up at me, then at the dish of apples.

"Here, have one," she says, fishing out a slice. I remember the taste of apples, the sour springing juice. She shakes it at me anxiously, glances at the trailer windows. For him to see this would mean a beating.

"I think I'm done," I say, and stand up.

12

The will to leave, the plan, accretes slowly, since it has been inconceivable, mentally forbidden, for so long. There's a girl in my gifted class sophomore year, friendly, mouthy. She's always been nice to me. Over weeks, in bits and pieces, I tell her — not about the visits to my room at night; they're nebulous, unreal, and perhaps I really am lying, making it up. But I tell her about the hitting, the hunger, and the endless work.

"Well, fuck that with a pitchfork," my friend says at the lunch table. "Get out of there."

I tell her I have nowhere to go.

She asks about possibilities, relatives, about my real father.

"No," I say quickly. "He's disfellowshipped."

"Dis-whatted?" Her face is scorn.

I try to explain. "It's like being excommunicated. He sinned and wasn't repentant. We have to shun him." She's not religious. She and her family are atheists, and when I try to witness to her, she rolls her eyes and tells me to shut up. It's part of what draws me to her, along with the swear words, which sound so pungent in a girl's mouth, a girl my age.

"What did he do?"

"He smokes cigarettes."

"Fuck that," she says. "Does he whale on you?"

I must look confused, because she sighs. "Hit you," she says patiently. "Does he hit you?"

"No. No, of course not."

"Does he hit your brother?"

"No."

"Beat your mom?"

I shake my head. I can't even picture it.

"Fuck it, then," she says. "What kind of a god gives more of a shit about smoking than somebody who whales on little kids?" She goes back to her sandwich. What kind of a god? My father would let me go to the Kingdom Hall; he did before.

"Look," she says, "if you ever want help getting out of that fuckhole, let me know."

In December, my grandmother sends — not wrapped for Christmas; she knows better — a pair of Nike tennis shoes, my size, nylon and leather, the color of cream, and a pair of Calvin Klein jeans, too loose but beautiful. For a year and a half, I've gone to high school in clothes out of garbage bags, ill-fitting polyester, ugly colors, old styles — starting school as the new kid again, this time visibly poor.

The shoes are soft and spongy inside, not like the cheap dimestore tennis shoes our mother buys us, and the jeans are thick cotton, dark indigo with coppery thread.

My stepfather tantrums up and down the trailer. These are worldly, materialistic clothes, flaunting their tags on the outside. Clothes that draw attention to themselves. No, he says. I cannot wear them to school. Not looking like that. I can wear them to do chores if I want. Vanity, vanity, all is vanity, he rants.

It's what I love about them, of course: what makes them contenders in the competitive parade of girls in high school, a competition I can't even enter. I say nothing, my eyes lowered to show obedience.

"You want her to waste them?" my mother intervenes. "We don't have the money to be wasting good clothes and shoes." Ordinarily she would balk on the jeans — I can see it in her face — but she says nothing. She wants me to have something nice.

He compromises. I can wear the clothes and shoes, he offers, if I remove all traces of their brands, all labels.

The jeans are a lost cause. There's no way to save the label; when I clip it from the pocket, the removal shreds its edges. Although the hallmark stitching pattern on the pockets is still there, people will think the jeans are knockoffs without the label. But the shoes have possibilities. I use an old bottle of my mother's Liquid Paper to paint over the *NIKE* on the leather heel pads. The label on the tongue, I cut free, flip underneath, and fasten with loose and tiny stitches on the inside.

I present it all for his inspection. He's sullen but concedes there's no trace left of a brand — Nike's swoosh isn't ubiquitous yet, so my stepfather doesn't recognize it, though I know people at high school will.

I pull on the jeans, thick and beautiful, and carry the shoes up the snowy road to the bus stop, a needle and thread hidden in the lining of my coat. On the forty-five-minute ride to school, I scrape away the Liquid Paper with my pen cap and restitch the labels in place on the tongues. As the bus bumps along, I hold them on my lap, heady with triumph, staring out the window without seeing. I've outwitted him.

At school I keep them in my locker, changing into them each morning like a positive pleasure. I walk down the halls like I'm walking on feathers, like the goddess of victory, airy and sure.

Snow beds deep on the frozen ground. It's a Saturday. The trees are sheathed in ice. Wind shrieks beneath the trailer, whipping between the cement blocks that support it. The water pipes, uninsulated, have frozen overnight.

Our stepfather sends us out to thaw them. Tony is given a hair dryer and an extension cord. My tool is a kettle of hot water. Each of us gets a flattened box to lie on, but we must cover the whole sixty-foot length of the trailer; we can drag the cardboard with us if we want, but it had better not slow us down. We cannot wear gloves. "Gloves make you slow, dummies. Clumsy and slow." No hats. No scarves. They'll get in the way.

In the low dark space under the trailer, we crawl, Tony aiming the dryer's nozzle at the plastic pipes, trailing the orange cord behind him. I drizzle hot water. When the kettle is empty, I crawl out, climb the portable wooden stairs, knock on the trailer door, and hand it to our mother. She shuts the door and disappears. The door opens again, and she gives me our other kettle, steaming. Then I crawl back below.

For hours, we maneuver between the stacked cement blocks, wiggling under PVC, over thick metal beams that span the trailer, avoiding the looping tangles of wires that nest above our heads, slowly dragging our bodies across the frozen mud. When I pass my brother, I look into his eyes.

"You okay?"

He nods. Snot is frozen to his lip. His eyelashes are frosted. The kettle empties again and again. We do not eat or drink. We may not use the bathroom until there's water to use.

When she opens the door, I can feel the heat fanning out against my face. Inside, the orange rug glows warm. The television is on. He's on the couch, forking pie into his mouth.

"You better hurry it up," he yells, his words distorted through food. He doesn't turn. The door shuts, and the air on my face is icy again. It opens, and her arm with the kettle extends. She doesn't look at me. "You better not spill no water," he calls, "unless you want punished." I crawl back under.

Sixty feet up, sixty feet back. There is a kind of dead feeling of endlessness. When I pass him, Tony's eyes are black tunnels in the gloom, and my fingers have become stiff greenish lumps, difficult to bend. Once when I take the steaming kettle from my mother, I stumble going down the stairs, and I automatically steady it so it will not spill. I see my bare hand against it, but there's no feeling of heat, not even of pressure. When I walk toward the place where my cardboard lies, my feet won't move the way I want them to. It's almost a relief to crouch down. My arm with the kettle shakes. When water spills on my fingers, a little steam rises.

Crawling, we know nothing but crawling. The whole world narrows to a dark space of frozen mud. I love to stand at the door when it is shut, because I know in a moment it will open, and the heat will come out, and my mother will look over my shoulder, and for this minute I do not have to move, just stand in the wind, ears throbbing. The sun lowers, a chilled white ball, dim, easy to look at.

In the gloom, we hear his heavy footfalls on the stairs. He has come out to inspect. The kettle's empty, and I crawl out.

"Don't you slow down, idiot," he yells to Tony. He walks the length of the trailer. I come back down the stairs, my kettle full. "Get on under there." I crawl onto my sodden cardboard. Our mother comes out, bundled up, her arms wrapped around her body. His voice raises so my brother can hear, too. "I guess you just ain't working hard enough," he says. "You're gonna have to stay out here till you get 'em unthawed." He hawks and spits. "I don't care how dark it gets, either. You ain't coming in till it's finished."

And then my body does something strange. I think, *I have to start crawling. I have to pour the water.* But I collapse instead on the cardboard, shuddering. I start to cry, and I hear myself crying, like hiccoughs, loud and open in the air. He kicks my foot. I just lie there, crying, not moving at all.

"I can't," I say. "I won't." I sob into the filthy cardboard like it's my friend. I'm certain he will kill me now, and I want him to. I am not crawling. I want him to shoot me with his rifle, now, right now, an end to it.

But his voice is soft, crooning, a voice like love. "Get up," he says. "Go in." I lie there for a minute more, his impossible words taking shape in my head. Never before has he let us stop because we're tired. I pull myself out and climb the stairs. I leave my brother there.

Inside, I stagger straight into the bathroom and bend my torso over the tub. My hand knocks upward against the faucet, and a clear, thick stream of hot water pours out. Steam coats my face and fills my open mouth. My hands begin vaguely to throb. Unmoving, I lie there in my coat and boots. The strange sobs fade and then cease. Our stepfather and mother come back into the trailer; their two sets of steps vibrate the floor as they head for the kitchen. There's an urgency in my brain, a chant: *He's still down there. He's littler. You have to get him. You have to go back down.* But I cannot move or speak. I've left him.

Perhaps ten minutes pass. Not long, but long enough for my feet to begin to hurt. In the living room, my stepfather says, "All right. Get the boy."

The door opens. My mother calls. It shuts. It opens and shuts again, and I hear his light steps coming down the hall.

"You can wash up even though she's in there," she says. His steps hesitate and then come closer, changing from the muffled sound on carpet to the squeak of wet rubber on linoleum.

I twist my shoulders to look up at him, but he doesn't look back.

He steps over me like you step over shit.

Moments of brokenness interest me. Everyone else seems to remember the egg-eating scene, but I'm hypnotized as Cool Hand Luke implodes in the hole he has dug and filled and redug to no purpose but the warden's pleasure at the breaking of his mind. I sit paralyzed, *1984* gripped open in my hands, as the rats chatter near Winston's face, as he cries, "Do it to Julia!" Released, he shows up at his old haunts, a shell of himself.

I would like to find myself compelled by images of death in triumph, by Mel Gibson trumpeting "Freedom!" as he's eviscerated and dies, by binary battlefields rich with the promise of honor. But I do not. They are too simple. They are, in a sense, convenient.

What is interesting is what happens when they will not let you die, when you are caught and kept alive beyond the point of breaking. How Luke, broken, still rallies and runs at the end of the movie. That knowledge always inside you of just how far you can be made to go and whom you will betray. But you keep running.

In small-town West Virginia, 1982, such things as homeless shelters, domestic violence shelters, do not exist. There might be homes for runaways, but I'm not allowed to look at the phone book, and I'm pretty sure my father won't want me now, after I've behaved so badly. I need to ask. But there's no way to reach him. The only places I go are to the Kingdom Hall and to school. I have no money, no way to make a long-distance call from the cafeteria pay phone.

My mouthy friend suggests using the phone at the guidance counselor's. But I can't imagine they would let me call for free. "Try it," says my friend. "Go ask, at least. What have you got to lose?" But I am terrified. I don't talk to people, don't ask for things. Just the thought makes my heart pound hard. I practice what I'll say silently at my locker, in my classes, on the bus.

When I stammer out my fragmented request to the woman sitting in the office, not looking her in the eye, she's quiet at first, a terrible, skeptical pause, so I outline what's happening, just briefly, just a sketch. I don't want another scene with my stepfather ordering me to recant, not here on school property. She crosses and uncrosses her navy loafers as I talk.

"Of course you can use my phone," she says finally, her voice sad. "Of course you can, dear." She gets up. "I'll give you a little privacy." She pushes the phone across the desk to me and moves to the door, then turns back. "But why didn't you come talk with me about all this?"

I look into her face; her eyes are sorrowful and kind. She seems nice. I can't tell her that psychology is a ploy of Satan, that she is deceived by the Devil and does the Devil's work. That I hardly talk to worldly people at all. "I don't know," I mumble. I look down at her loafers, which slowly turn and disappear.

I dial information for my father's number at work and write it down on the memo pad. My finger shakes on its way to press each number. I say a quick prayer that he hasn't left his job.

I ask for him by name and then wait as the hold music plays. Violins, violins. My whole body trembles in the chair. What if he hangs up?

"This is Lee Castro." His voice is confident, businesslike, sure. Tears rush into my eyes at the sound of it, the first time I've heard it in over a year. It sounds just the same. This is the voice I know, the voice that will always be there. "Hello?" he says. "Hello?"

"Dad?" My voice is small, tinny, a voice in a cup or from the bottom of a well.

"Honey?" he says. *"Joy?"*

"Dad." It's all I can say.

"Oh, God," I hear him say, the phone away from his mouth. "Oh, Jesus. It's my kid." He sounds choked. "Can you give me a minute?" he says to someone in the room. A pause. "No, you don't understand. It's my kid. I need a minute." Another pause, and then his voice is louder, more desperate. "Look, would you just get out, please?" A door closes.

"Honey?" he says. "Honey?" He's crying. "Honey, are you okay?"

All that evening and night I am afraid — that the guidance counselor will have called the trailer, trying to be helpful; that my mother or stepfather, uncanny, will somehow ask a question that I'll have to answer, which will give the plan away. Driving home in the snow from the book-study that night, he lectures long on loyalty: to The Truth, to one's family, and I tremble in the backseat, waiting for him to pounce. But it's nothing, just one more routine lecture.

The next morning, I rise at five as usual and pull on my best summer pants, light as a breath, and then, over them, the jeans my grandmother has given me. I slip two thin shirts on under a sweater, and then a heavier sweater. At the breakfast table, my mother doesn't notice the extra bulk. Together with the Nikes in my locker, it's everything I will take.

Outside it is freezing and still dark. The snow is packed; the road and fields glow white. Glittering ice coats the trees. The bus stop is a mile away; they've clocked it with the Scout, so my stepfather can insist to my mother that it's not too far for children to walk. All the way, I ask my brother if he could bear to live with our father.

"No," he says woodenly each time. "He's disfellowshipped. You know that."

"This isn't a test," I plead. "I won't tell on you, no matter what you answer. I just really need to know." If he just says yes, we can pick him up, too. Otherwise, it would be kidnapping. The lawyer will have two versions of the papers ready: one for just me, one for both of us. But he's adamant, shaking his head. I look into his eyes, trying to convince him that it's safe, it's me — this isn't one more trap that leads to the belt.

I can't tell him. I can't say, "Dad's picking me up at three, and he has a thing signed by the judge, and I'm going to live with him, but I'll still be in The Truth. I'll still go to meetings. He said I could." Because if my brother walks straight into the elementary school and tells the teacher he has to call his mom, it's an emergency, and she and my stepfather find out before I'm safely in another county hours away with legal papers, I do not know what will happen, what explosion in my school, my stepfather bursting into biology class to drag me away by the arm and take me to the trailer, how he will make sure I never have another chance.

So I beg, trying not to sound urgent, all the way to the bus stop and then all the forty-five minutes over gravel roads and then paved roads until we get to town, but he is as firm as the wall we've been told to be like — like the Shulamite Maiden, sure and faithful and committed — repeating everything we've been drilled in about how Satan the Devil can be anywhere, anytime, how he can tempt you, how he can look like an angel of light if he wants. He glares at me when he says that. When the bus shudders to a stop at the grade school, he shrugs away out of the seat, angry. He thinks I'm testing him. My forehead against the icy glass, I watch through the window as he mounts the stairs to the school's brick archway, his steps resolute, his little back hunched. Then the bus moves away, and I can't see him anymore.

That afternoon, my father picks me up from school. When I come out, there is his red Monza, and he's getting out of it, and I'm in his arms, and then we are driving fast to be out of the county before I would have ordinarily gotten home. His attorney calls my mother to notify her that my legal transfer has occurred. I wait, tense, for an explosion, for my stepfather to burst out from behind a wall with his gun. But nothing happens.

That night, the phone rings at my father's house. He answers it. It's my mother for me, he says, but when I get to the phone, it's my stepfather's voice that's talking.

"Do you agree to release me from all responsibility as your spiritual father?" he says. My hand has started to shake at the sound of his voice.

"What?" I'm not sure what's happening, what it means.

"Do you, or do you not, agree to release me from all responsibility as your spiritual father? All responsibility for your spiritual upbringing?"

"I guess so."

"Don't get smart with me, God damn it. Just say you do or you don't."

"I do."

The line goes dead. And that's it. It's that simple.

13

At my father's little green rented house, I pray for Tony. I think every day of how to get him out. I write to him, wondering if he'll get my letters.

I don't have enough clothes to start the new school year, so my father and stepmother take me to Gabriel's. It's just an outlet store, since I'll need so much, they say apologetically, but to me, it looks wonderful. With its wide tables, crowded with overstocks and items flawed during manufacturing, it seems like a bazaar in some exotic land. I keep running my hands over the jumbled stacks of T-shirts. Lilac, yellow, white, everything soft and brand-new and clean. When I try things on, my father and stepmother sit just outside on metal folding chairs, laughing at the way my feet dance below the dressing-room door. I choose khakis and blue jeans and pale-colored button-down shirts, everything a little loose, a kind of unobtrusive uniform, and a pair of brown topsiders like I've seen in *Seventeen*. They buy me a new coat that fits.

I call my grandmother, my mother's mother, to let her know I'm all right and why I ran away. She cries on the phone and says she is glad, she has been so worried. Now we just need to get Tony out of there, she says.

My stepmother takes me to a salon where a woman puts the right colors of blush and lipstick on my face. We buy the little compacts and brushes. Then we go to her hairdresser's shop, all warmth and shampoo. Everyone is nice to me, gentle. They call me by name and say how nice it is to meet me.

I keep thanking my father and stepmother, who say to stop, it's all right. They look like they're on the verge of tears.

My father makes a fake version of his company newsletter, with a Polaroid of me on the front and the airline's company logo at the top. *Joy Castro Returns Home,* it says. He writes a funny little article about the ticker-tape parade that accompanies my return.

When I wake up with nightmares, my stepmother sits on the edge of my bed and strokes my hair until I fall back to sleep.

At the new school, I try hard not to be noticed.

When I was little, my father called me beautiful, but once I move in, adolescent, gaunt, gray-faced, he says nothing. I eat like a wolf: tuna sandwiches, slices of wheat bread straight out of the bag, milk, orange juice. I begin to grow taller, add pounds. My hair turns glossy and bright.

I cannot seem to stop eating. If my belly empties and growls, I become anxious. There's something about chewing, about the food crumbling and moistening, moving inside my mouth, that calms me.

The first letter from my mother arrives. It rewrites my running away into a story about betraying her, about wanting a life of worldly pleasures.

> My Dear Joy:
>   Remember I told you that there is a special something between a girl and her mother that no one or thing

could ever destroy? Well, I guess I was wrong. I should have said there's a special something that a mother has for her daughter that no one can ever destroy. I guess daughters don't always have this special something for their mothers but mothers do for their daughters, at least I do for you and my mother did for me.

Daughters, though have a way of kicking their mothers right in the stomach (or heart) to take the wind out of them for awhile, but mothers, true to form, usually bounce back and continue thinking of their daughters as a special someone to love always and to share a deep bond with no matter who else enters their lives. My mother is right now still holding her stomach, thanks to your phone call (that was the lowest, hardest blow of it all — for you to ^try to destroy the bond between us and then the bond between me and my mother, and I'd be hard to convince it was your idea — only one person could come up with as damaging an incident as that). I hurt my mother once before like that, when I left home. I was 18. I never realized how badly I hurt my mother until now. But, daughters have a way of finding out too late what it's like to be a mother. You were able to move and find another mother, maybe better, but I will never want or have any other daughter but you.

I don't know what is coming next but I want you to know I understand what you did. I don't approve and I don't like it but I understand. I hope you are happy and enjoy life with your family. Live it to the full as they do because when it's over it will be all there is. 1 Cor. 15:32

I'm sorry I failed you in what you want out of life and I guess I failed Jehovah in what he expected me to do for you, but despite my failures you will always have a very special place in my heart, my life and my love,
Mom
3 John 4

I look up the scriptures. The Corinthians scripture is that one about worldly people who eat, drink, and are merry, for tomorrow they shall die. The one in John reads, "No greater cause for thankfulness do I have than these things, that I should be hearing that my children go on walking in the truth."

I tear the letter's three sheets neatly one way and then the other. Then I tear up the envelope.

I go to all the meetings and out in service. I sit alone in the Kingdom Hall, knowing no one. A middle-aged sister studies the truth book with me once a week so I can prepare for baptism. I'm fourteen; it's time.

We study in her living room. Her husband is a stiff, graying elder who always wears a suit. Grooves run from the corners of his mouth down to his jawline, like a marionette's, and his forehead looks angry all the time, even when he's saying something innocuous. Their grown-up son seems nervous and shy, sort of flinchy. But the sister is sweet and pale, a tall, fleshy woman with a high voice and a big brown mole the size of a button on her cheek. Her lips are painted bright pink, and her eyeliner is thick and careful. Her hair dye is too dark for her skin. She looks like a man dressed up like a woman, and her high voice sounds like a falsetto. She's sweet, and I feel sorry for her.

My father says we might have to wait until Tony's fourteen, too — the age at which a child's testimony counts in the eyes of the law.

But we can't wait. My father doesn't understand. There's no way he can stay there five years.

My mother's letters come regularly, each paragraph ending with a scriptural citation like the paragraphs in the Watchtower's books: *We read your letter out loud as a family when we received it. It sounds as though you are really living high and free. Proverbs 29:15b.* She upbraids me, mentioning my brother's hard work on the land and the Witnesses she's seen recently. She lets me know I'm replaceable, rubbing it in, saying of the pretty majorette who now dates Tommy Singleton, *We've been taking pictures of her as we needed someone about your age. You would have been perfect for the assignment but we were happy to get her as she works well in front of the camera.*

She mentions Rebecca Hinton, a little girl from the Kingdom Hall. I remember her: thin and quiet, about nine, my brother's age, with pale skin and white-blond hair clinging limply to her skull, her brothers Isaiah and Zechariah, big-eyed, skinny children who never let go of their Bibles. *We have been taking Rebecca out in service with us almost every weekend lately and hope to have her spend the night. . . . We've been taking a lot of pictures of her lately and the Agency in New York has kept several.* I know there's no *we* about it; that my step-father takes the pictures, that my mother's not even in the room. And we were never allowed to have friends sleep over in the trailer before, so why a little girl?

There's never anything from my brother, but from time to time, she encloses a note from my stepfather.

> DON'T FAINT BECAUSE I'M WRITING. AS YOU KNOW I DO NOT WRITE (OR PRINT) LETTERS TO ANYONE BUT I JUST HAD TO LET YOU KNOW THAT I LOVE YOU + WANT YOU TO BE HAPPY.
>
> I WAS GLAD TO HEAR THAT YOU ARE ATTEND-ING MEETINGS + GOING OUT IN SERVICE + I HOPE THAT SOMEDAY YOU WILL BE MY SISTER.
>
> AS I WRITE I CAN THINK OF A LOT OF THINGS I WOULD LIKE TO SAY BUT FOR NOW I'LL JUST SAY THAT JEHOVAH WILL TAKE GOOD CARE OF YOU IF YOU LOVE HIM ABOVE EVERYONE + EVERY THING ELSE.
>
> P.S. I MISS MY LITTLE GIRL.

At school, I make a friend, a boy who tells me people think I'm stuck-up because of the way I never talk and walk with my back very straight. This comes as a jolt that fascinates: the extreme disjunction that can exist between people's perceptions of you and how you actually are inside. But I decide it's better this way: better to be thought haughty than scared. Besides, I have other things on my mind. I don't want my brother to spend another summer there, when our stepfather will have little to do but dream up ways to occupy and torment him. Before school lets out for the summer, I develop a plan. My father discusses it with his lawyer, who agrees that it could work and prepares the same kind of document he prepared for me before I ran away. And one very warm, bright day, my father drives me to the high school where I used to go. When my old school bus comes, I get on with a note. It heads toward the elementary school.

Things get dim and fragmented then, bright bursts of color and action, the links between them difficult to recall.

IN THE CIRCUIT COURT OF HARRISON COUNTY,
WEST VIRGINIA

My mother,
   Plaintiff,

  vs.   *CIVIL ACTION NO. 78-C-205-2*
LIBANO F. CASTRO,

                 Defendant

Four numbered paragraphs give the background of the case, describing the divorce and the custody agreement. And then:

> 5. *On June 2, 1982, the Petitioner, at the request of Joy Castro, took Joy Castro to Buckhannon, West Virginia, so that she would have an opportunity to visit with her brother.* My father follows in his red hatchback, stopping when the bus stops. *Both children rode a school bus for some time, not in the presence of the Petitioner.* The way my brother's face lights up when he gets on at the grade school, sees me in the green seat halfway back. The way he rushes toward me where I wait, unsure of his reaction, my breath coming fast. How he hugs me, smiling, and won't let go,

even to put down his book bag. How he wants right away to come with me. *At the instruction of the Petitioner, Joy Castro was to disembark from the school bus prior to reaching the home of the Plaintiff and was to return with the Petitioner to his home.*

It's important that the legal document omit mention of any pre-meditated plan that he leave, claiming that I only wanted to visit. For some legal reason, the impulse to leave has to come from my brother alone to be valid.

6. *At the agreed location, both children left the school bus.* As we run to our father's idling car, a Styrofoam cup slips from Tony's hands, bursts, and tears open on the asphalt. The little plant lies in its soil, and he crouches over it to scoop it back up. "Leave it," I say. "We've got to hurry." The car is waiting; the school bus has driven on; in thirty minutes they will know; we don't have long. We need to be in another part of the state, with legal papers and police, before they realize what's happened. But he wants the little plant that he has grown from a seed in the schoolroom, that he has watered and watched and put on the windowsill with the other children's. He has lettered his name with blue pencil on the Styrofoam rim, and a green shoot has pushed up. He wants to save it. I am fourteen and terrified; I grab his hand and pull him. "Come on," I say. "It doesn't matter. We'll get you another one." He comes. *The Petitioner's son informed the Petitioner that he no longer desired to remain with the Plaintiff and her current husband, but desired to live with the Petitioner and his sister.* In the car, my father laughs and cries at once. *Said son refused to go to the Plaintiff's home and on advice of counsel, the Petitioner permitted his son to remain with him.*

7. *The Petitioner is informed and believes and on such information and belief alleges that his attorney immediately attempted to contact the Plaintiff to inform her of the circumstances and*

notify her that said son was safe and with his father. The Petitioner alleges that his attorney was unable to contact the Plaintiff but did inform her husband of the circumstances — he no longer allowed my mother to answer or use the telephone — *and of the desire of the Petitioner's son to remain with the Petitioner.*

My father drives fast until we're out of the county. We go to the lawyer's office, just as we had when I ran away, and pick up my step-mother from work. We eat McDonald's on the bare floor of the new house we're buying, larger than the little rental house, so my brother and I will have plenty of room. At every step, there's hugging and crying. My brother is waif-thin, with dark circles under his eyes. Under his clothes, there are bruises, as there always are. His face is hollow and fragile, but happy now.

Probably our stepfather will call tonight, as he did when I ran away, but other than that, we're home free. It's late afternoon when we pull into the driveway of the green rental house, all together at last.

8. *Upon arrival at his home, the Plaintiff and her husband were awaiting the Petitioner.* "Lock the doors, lock the doors," Tony whimpers as soon as we see the Scout in our driveway, quickly pressing his lock and our father's down, rolling up his window. My father and his wife sit frozen, stunned, as if they cannot comprehend what's happening. But we know. I smack down the locks on my side. "Drive," I say. "Drive. Hurry. Put it in reverse." But my father does not drive. I roll my window up, and my brother hunches low in his seat, crying, as our stepfather moves toward us, his thick bulk coming fast down the driveway. He *physically removed Tony from the vehicle of the Petitioner and physically forced him to return to Buckhannon.* While our father says something about the law, our stepfather's thick arm sails through his open window and flips up

the lock on the back door. He opens it and plucks my brother up, carries him by his upper arm, dangling in the air — Tony's free hand reaching back toward us — to the Scout, and throws him in the backseat. *During this time, the Plaintiff was physically abusing Joy Castro who is by Order of this Court in the care, custody and control of the Petitioner.* "Give me my son!" my mother screams, unlocking my door through our step-mother's open front window, opening my door, hurling herself against my body, reaching across me for my brother, clawing, slapping my arms and face. "Give me my son!" She screams it even after my brother is gone. Tony twists around in the Scout, screaming, but I can't hear him. I see his eyes through the space and the layers of glass that separate us, and suddenly my mother is in the Scout, and then they are gone. I stagger out and stand on the grass in the late afternoon sun, screaming a hoarse and hollow scream.

Taken, subscribed and sworn to before me this 3rd day of June, 1982.

For three months afterward, our lives are a series of petitions, depositions, and hearings. I practice my testimony in my bedroom. I might have to testify in judge's chambers, or I might not. The lawyer might put me on the stand, or he might not.

We learn from the police that my stepfather successfully impersonated a Marion County deputy sheriff in order to find out where we live. "That asshole," the real sheriff keeps saying. He offers to testify. "That completely insane asshole."

I know no limits will stop him. In dreams my stepfather vaults up to the witness stand, over benches and past court officials, to seize and throttle me.

People mill about, waiting for the judge. I sit between my father and our lawyer, stroking the soft blue fabric of my new dress. The courthouse is pretty, all gleaming brown wood and old-fashioned moldings, lamps, swirling tile mosaics on the floor, and I try to think about that.

My mother and her husband enter the courtroom, and he glares at me. People's voices dim to an echoey hush. My body starts to tremble. He sits down, but she stays standing. Tony isn't with them. She stares at me, holding out her arms, smiling.

"Aren't you going to come here?" she says. People turn to look. I get up and walk over to her. A low wooden wall, the height of our hips, divides us. Her arms stay stretched in the air, prongs of flesh. I look at them oddly; the last time I saw them, they were hitting me. The last time I saw her, I was only an obstacle, not human, not her daughter. "Aren't you going to hug your own mother?" she says loudly. Guilt wells up in me like vomit. I tilt forward and put my arms around her. I feel like a mechanical doll; I think I may tip over. Her body feels stiff and strange, upholstered. She hugs me tightly.

I go back to my seat and the judge starts talking. The lawyers talk. I can't stop yawning. Everything blurs by.

Later in the echoing hallway, during a recess, my father is angry. "How could you do it?" he asks in a hoarse whisper. The lawyer shakes his head. Hugging my mother like that, demonstrating affection. Whose side am I on? The judge will interpret it as a sign of sympathy for her. Don't I know anything about how this all works?

"I do have sympathy for her," I say. "He beats her too, you know." My father looks away.

It drags on, a complicated case: hearsay, conflicting testimony, and again the issues of a mother's rights, of religious freedom.

Finally, our lawyer says in court that he will put me on the stand. I will tell everything I know. It's unusual, a fourteen-year-old, but this is an unusual case.

I can't eat. In my imagination, I practice looking at my mother's face, my stepfather's glassy eyes, while telling what happens there. I keep stopping the vision of my stepfather roaring toward me, but again and again in my mind's eye, he rises from his pew.

We get a call the next day: with no contest, my brother will be ready to be transferred a few days later, in August, six months after I have run away.

The threat of putting me on the stand, our lawyer crows, has done the trick. He knew it; it has been his trump card all along.

The day my brother moves in, my father smokes his last cigarette.

For a long time after I become an adult, I remember only the flight and what followed: how my brother and I made our way in the world, the little fires he set in the closet under the stairs, the boys I fucked, the drugs we took as we got older, the way we forged some kind of eventual life, how for years I would have no Bible in my house. How for some time the only things on the walls of his rented room were a postcard I sent him, a mask I fired in college, a photograph of us together, but how he never answered messages I left. That little room lit by the great silent tank, bubbling and clean, alive with plants and fish rescued from drying rock pools, its glass cube big as his own twin bed, its coverlet brown and somber as a monk's. The scars that laced his hands like fretwork: burn-scars, cut-scars, his hands plunged into engines all day. You fix them, they function. No surprises.

I am thirty-three when I wake choking from a dream of the little plant. A small green seedling, the one thing he wanted to take with him. Alone in the brightness of my room, I see how simple it would have been to have helped him scoop it up, to have held it in our hands together as we rushed to the revving car. How you can be saying to someone, "You are the most important person in the world to me," and yet be ignoring the small thing closest to his heart. How you can halo yourself as the hero and never match up the shards that say you're not. How quickly it all happens and then there is no way back.

14

When Tony arrives, they let us lie in their big bed and watch movies on TV. It's a heated waterbed, a California king as wide as it is long, with four wooden pillars and a flat wooden roof lined inside with six mirrors. A seventh mirror runs up the center of the headboard, flanked by brown leather pads. A theme park of a bed, it has always fascinated us, from the time we first saw it during visitation years ago — when, excited, we told our mother about it back home, and heard her bitter laugh. Now we spend hours there, like in a nest or cave. The sheets have little jungle animals on them: elephants, lions, giraffes. Everything is warm and brown.

We are hypnotized by the vision of ourselves in the mirrors, the rippling warmth of it, the pillows stuffed with down, softer than any pillows we've felt before. We watch *The Muppet Movie, Superman,* Disney cartoons. Childish, comforting movies. They take us to the movie theater, out to dinner. We make friends at school.

For a few months, my brother and I go to the Kingdom Hall together — our father drives us — and out in service. But even though I'm living with an apostate, I don't feel damned, or like Jehovah hates me. Christmas seems innocent and pretty, not wicked. I keep studying the truth book with the middle-aged sister, but its reasons still don't make sense, and there's no one to shut me up about it now. When I tell her I won't be coming for my weekly Bible study anymore, she cries. She wants me to pray with her and hold hands. They're broad and ringed, puffed with flesh and powdery, with little bright pink painted tips. She prays on and on, her eyes shut, crying. I watch her eyeliner melt. A drip of it runs down to her mole. I feel sad, but I don't go back.

We never talk with my father and stepmother about what happened in the trailer, except to make jokes. After we stop going to the Kingdom Hall, we pass it sometimes in the car.

"Christmas!" we yell out the window. "Birthdays!" "Fun!" Tony adds, grinning a version of his old grin. This is acceptable, cathartic. We yell and laugh about it. Our father is comfortable with this.

But we don't talk about what happened. When I start to, his face closes. "That's all over now, honey," he says quickly, sternly. He doesn't want to hear it. He pats my shoulder in a firm way.

We keep it to ourselves.

Once early on, he takes us to a counselor, and Tony and I sit there for an hour, stony, still distrustful of psychologists. Our father has made it plain that, in his view, they are for the weak. When he asks if I want to go back, I say I don't.

"Then everything must be fine," he says, smiling.

In February, 1983, one year after I ran away, the story breaks across the state.

Photographer Is Charged, the headlines read. *Sheriff Helps Nab Photographer In Sexual Abuse of Child Case. Sex Abuse Trial Set. Photographer Gets Molesting Charge. Child Molesting Charges Filed. Accused Photographer Obtains Ban on Photos During Court Session.*

My father hires a news clipping service to keep up with all the articles, wedged in among headlines that read, *Wadestown Man Elected to Top Shriners' Post, Snowstorm Effects Still Being Felt on Roads,* and *Cannelton Will Reopen Some Mines.* (At the top of one page, an article, dateline Jerusalem, opens: *A defiant Defense Minister Ariel Sharon resisted mounting pressure for his resignation today over the Beirut massacre commission's ruling that he bore personal responsibility for the refugee camp slaughter.*) The clipping service sends the UPI version in dot-matrix all-caps with its preface: *BROADCAST-ERS: NOTE SEXUAL NATURE THROUGHOUT.*

The clippings, pieced together, tell the story.

According to Tucker County Sheriff Darl Pine, our stepfather, whom the newspapers called *a freelance photographer, came to Tucker County last fall and advertised for models to pose for him.*

"He set up a photo session at Carl's Motel just outside of Parsons and began making calls to homes in the area," Pine said.

Darl Pine, Carl's Motel — the strangely backwoods sound of the names, like a parody, ridiculous, something sordid for city people to lampoon.

On one of these calls our stepfather *allegedly talked the mother of the young girl into allowing him to be alone with her daughter in her upstairs bedroom in order that the two "could become better acquainted," Pine said.*

Or, *"During the first incident on Oct. 6,* he *had gone to this family's home and asked the mother to leave the room so that the girl could get used to him and feel comfortable around him,"* said the prosecuting attorney, *indicating that this is when the sexual abuse occurred which he defined as "intercourse or the touching of the mouth to sex organs" and in this case* the attorney *said it was the touching of the mouth to sex organs. He defined abuse as "no intercourse is involved . . . it is the touching of sex organs."*

"When he left, the girl broke down crying and told her mother what had happened," the sheriff said.

The girl's mother reported the incident to Pine, who succeeded in getting charges brought against the photographer on Oct. 6, 1982, without our stepfather's *knowledge.*

"We knew when it got to court it would be a 9-year-old vs. a 42-year-old," Pine explained, "so we kept it quiet."

The prosecutor said the girl told her mother but it was the child's word against that of my stepfather. That was when the surveillance by the sheriff was set up, he said.

Little nine-year-old Hambledon or Hambleton girl, how could they have made you go through it again? What did your mother and the sheriff say? That it was the only way to catch him? "I spent three or four hours with the mother and child trying to build up the girl's confidence," said Pine.

The sheriff hid in a closet for nearly two hours in order to observe our stepfather and the girl. Pine said that when our stepfather "did some pretty disgusting things" he burst out of the closet and he "found himself looking down the barrel of my .357 magnum."

Or, in more detail: "He took a few pictures of the girl that were decent," Pine said, "then he did a few things that I did not think were correct, but that I did not think warranted a felony arrest."

About an hour and 45 minutes into the photo session, the girl reportedly complained of being sick. Our stepfather apparently started rubbing her back, but stopped when the girl told him that it was her stomach that hurt.

"When he pulled her nightgown up and touched her, that's all I needed," Pine said.

Or, in another version, Sheriff Pine spent one hour and 45 minutes in a bedroom closet on the second floor of the family's two-story home observing the photographer. "The closet was very small and was covered by a curtain from which I could observe" him.

"He did some pretty disgusting things but as soon as he laid his hand on the girl's vagina I came out of the closet," said the sheriff, "and our stepfather found himself looking down the barrel of my .357 magnum."

The high melodrama of the ah-ha moment. The sheriff's lack

of anatomical accuracy. The weird humor in the sheriff's coming out of a literal closet.

"People don't think that things can happen here, but they need to know that it can!" Sheriff Pine said Monday morning.

Our stepfather *was arrested on the spot and charged with a second count of sexual abuse.* Little did anyone know that he was also *reportedly under investigation by Randolph County police authorities when he was arrested in Tucker County. He has also advertised for similar photo sessions in the Buckhannon area,* where we had lived in the trailer, *in the past, without apparent incident* — though we later learned that, once articles about the molesting charge appeared in papers throughout the state, more than one sexually assaulted woman came forth, offering to testify about her own photo sessions.

In one account, our stepfather was *in Randolph County jail, in lieu of $10,000 bond*; in another, the county magistrate *set bond at $10,000 on each count.* In some papers, they are *two counts of first-degree sexual abuse*; in others, they are one count *of first-degree sexual assault* and one of *first-degree sexual abuse.*

A desire for visual privacy could seem ironic, coming from someone *charged with setting up a "scam" as a freelance photographer* who *placed ads in newspapers advertising to go into homes to take photographs of girls and women — everything from models to grandmothers.*

Nonetheless, our stepfather wanted no cameras at his trial: *The lawyer for a freelance photographer accused in a Tucker County sexual abuse case wants his defendant to be the only cameraman in the courtroom during preliminary hearings.* The judge *opened the hearing by announcing that the Elkins Inter-Mountain newspaper had requested permission to take pictures during the proceedings, under guidelines laid down by the Supreme Court permitting cameras in the courtroom,* but the defense lawyer *objected strenuously.*

"I feel that there already has been undue media exposure based on an article that appeared in the Inter-Mountain on Feb. 9," he said, call-

ing the piece *"inflammatory."* He didn't believe our stepfather could *get a fair trial in Tucker County or other counties where the story has run.*

"I have not been able to look at the Charleston Gazette or Daily Mail, but I understand that they have picked up on this also," the defense lawyer said. He *said he was "concerned by cases, like this one, that are tried in the media."*

The press service sends us the originating ad, sandwiched between *FOR SALE — Jersey milk cow* and *FOR SALE — Hoover vacuum with Powermatic head, $25.* Just a little ad, the kind I saw him write with our mother, its rhetoric familiar:

> MODELS WANTED — For commercials any age, from babies to grandparents. No experience necessary. Apply in person only, Fri., Oct. 1 from 1 to 9 P.M. Carl's Motel Room No. 9. This could be your big chance. Don't miss it.

Five months later, another clipping arrives. *Photographer Faces Jail on Morals Count,* the headline reads.

A Buckhannon man has pleaded guilty to a first-degree sexual abuse charge after authorities accused him of posing as a professional photographer and then molesting a 9-year-old girl during a "modeling session," a court official says.

A grand jury initially charged him with first-degree sexual assault and first-degree sexual abuse. He pleaded guilty to the sexual abuse charge under a plea bargain.

The maximum sentence for the sexual abuse charge is 1-to-5 years in the state penitentiary and a $10,000 fine.

The name of the victim was not released.

I have no way to thank that unnamed girl, nine and brave — and her mother, who believed her — for going through with it, for generating the public record that corroborates my private truth, that proves I was not crazy, not lying, not imagining things.

Although I do not speak of what had happened to me — not then, and not for years — I have that mental satisfaction. Though something was missing, still — some vital piece, a blank place nagging at me — I can be certain that something had happened.

15

The beauty of every woman he sees, my father rates. He says it warmly, objectively, like a judge holding up a number in which the women should take pride. It's new to me, and intimidating. I don't know if he has changed, or if our aging has changed the way he acts around us, or if growing older has changed the way I view what had always been there, invisible to my younger self. I wonder if he did this with my mother, and what it did to her. I'd thought everything was going to be all right now, but the father I've moved in with is different from the father who took me out to breakfast as a child.

"Now, she's a lovely girl," he says in a low, glad voice as the waitress moves away from our table. "Don't you think?"

I stare at him. "I wasn't thinking about it."

He looks perturbed, nearly offended. "Well, next time, *look*," he says.

Fugly, he and his wife, who'd been a photographer's model in Chicago, call the unattractive women we see. Fat and ugly.

"Now, she's strangely attractive," he muses, as if contemplating a bone drawn from his lips. This is code for: She doesn't fit the convention of beauty defined by the stack of *Playboy*s that sit on his

181

toilet tank, but there's something hot about her. "Strangely attractive." Big nose, but curvy. Or too skinny, but with flirty eyes.

At home, when he can't hear us, Tony and I joke about it. "Now, there's a strangely attractive chest of drawers," I say, flopped on his bed, my eyes narrowed and lips bunched like a wine critic on TV.

"Ah, yes," he replies. "And have you noticed my strangely attractive ceiling fan?"

I make a new friend, a cheerleader with blond Farrah-hair and eyes the blue of swimming pools, the sort of girl who used to hate me. Secretly, she dates the assistant football coach and other grown-up men, divorced men with alimony payments. In chemistry class, she passes me notes about how giving head is like swallowing six eggs one after the other until you think you're going to suffocate but then they'll give you anything you ask for. When I bring her home, my father thinks she is a charming girl.

She throws up to make weight for the squad. It's easy; we eat lunch outside on the rail with the popular people and then vomit together, down in the basement girls' room at the high school.

When I spend the night at her house, we have the place to ourselves. Her mother works the night shift, and her father's dead — killed himself when she was twelve, girls say. She found him on her bed when she got home from school. But maybe it's just a rumor. She never brings it up, and part of the contract of my getting to be her friend is that I never mention it.

Orgies of chocolate ice cream ribbon from our mouths into the toilet bowl.

My father is an expert in Transactional Analysis: "I'm okay, you're okay." He learned it, and then he started giving seminars to airline employees, so they could get along better and be more productive. It's the perfect way, he says, for me to manage my inappropriate emotions.

So I read the dopey book, study the little circle diagrams. Big deal. In every situation, you have three options: to act like the Parent, the Child, or the Adult — the Adult being the rational, clearheaded, non-needy, unemotional, and highly superior part of you. If you let your Adult do the talking at work, everything goes smoothly. If other employees try to trap you into some dynamic to fulfill their Child needs or Parent needs, just remain in Adult mode, and their attempts will collapse.

My father is always the Adult, even at home. He's always in charge, always correct, calm, and stern. Sure, he can have fun — he has a reputation for being fun at work, always cracking a joke — but he's always an Adult. Always a professional, underneath the smile. When I was little, he seemed different. Now his softness is reserved only for his wife. He's absorbed in her.

Around the house, he manages my brother and me. Sometimes, I feel like there's no real person there. He doesn't show any emotions, ever, except exasperation when we don't fall in line — and even then, he doesn't take it personally; it's just a failure of ours to do what's expected. There's a slick, cheerful emptiness in his voice when he talks to us.

This is supposed to be the happy house, and it seems lonely and fake. When I tell him I don't like it, he's cool with me, managerial, like I'm some little bump in the road of his evening routine. He's very rational as he explains the way I need to look at things.

"Stop it," I say. "You're doing it. You're doing that stuff on me."

He says, "Well, you're letting your Child be in control."

"I *am* a child."

He sighs.

A letter comes from the penitentiary addressed to me. The cheap stationery is a long vertical wash of green grass. In the top margin, there's a rippling blue lake, a brown horse with its nose in the water, drinking. Hovering in the grass is a preprinted poem in tiny type called "A Tribute to your Friendship," the kind that rhymes. But I go straight to the writing, the familiar wavery all-caps.

> DEAR JOY
> I HOPE THIS NOTE FINDS YOU WELL AND HAPPY
> I KNOW THAT TO SAY IM SORRY WILL NOT MAKE THINGS BETTER
> BUT IT MAY HELP JUST A LITTLE.
> THE HORSE + POEM SEEMD SO RIGHT FOR YOU AND TRULY THE WAY I FEEL ABOUT YOU, I THOUGHT ID LET YOU KNOW. I HOPE IT DOESN'T OFFEND YOU TO HEAR FROM ME THIS WAY, BECAUSE ILL ALWAYS THINK OF YOU AS A BELOVED DAUGHTER EVERYDAY

And his signature, with his address.

> P.S. ID LIKE TO HEAR FROM YOU
> PEN PAL STYLE.

With one emendation, the little preprinted poem reads:

> Today, as I evaluate
> The joys ~~this~~ LAST year has brought
> It's not surprising in the least
> You fill my every thought—
> Because you see, high on the list
> Of things I'm grateful for
> Is friendship that you've given me
> And really, so much more—
> So please accept my thankfulness
> And may life always be
> As wonderful and kind to you
> As you have been to me.

And really, so much more.

*   *   *

In school, I am perpetually confused. How could people have crossed to the Americas forty thousand years ago — before humans were even created?

I am upset to learn that slavery happened so recently; I'd thought black people were enslaved in America around the time the Israelites were enslaved by the Egyptians. I am stunned to learn that racism exists, I have been so sheltered from it: the pictures in the Watchtower books, the multiracial Kingdom Halls. I have never heard a racist joke or remark.

The teachers and students are so blasé about it all. The immediacy of history shocks me — the timeline, clear and orderly, dispelling the blur in my head — as does the fact that I could have blocked out so much.

My father is driving me home from somewhere, just the two of us in his little red Monza. I am fifteen and incensed about nuclear war, which we've been discussing in class and which, without the certainty of Jehovah's intervention, is suddenly real and terrifying.

I ask why everyone isn't doing something about it, every day, until all the governments agree to dismantle their arms. Naive, I want to know why my father, in particular, isn't protesting — how he can live with knowing, every day, that his life — that *our* lives, his children's — could end in an instant: all of history, all of culture, all the things he loves.

"It can't happen," he says. "There will never be a nuclear war."

We argue fruitlessly.

"Look, Joy, it cannot happen here in America." His voice is stern, but then it drops to a slightly lower key, as if quoting: "There has never been a foreign war on American soil," he says. His tone lightens. "So you can stop worrying about it." He pulls into our driveway and turns off the motor with an air of finality. "We're the most powerful nation in the world. Countries depend on our goodwill. No one's going to bomb us."

"I don't understand how you can be so *calm* about all this. I don't understand why you're not *doing* something about it."

"Honey," he says with an edge, "what do you want me to do? I'm not a politician, I'm not a—"

"You could write to them. You could call the White House. You could get people together and go on a march."

"That's ridiculous. Where am I going to get the time to do all that? And who's going to listen to me? I'm nobody." He opens his door and turns toward me, his face like stone. "You get this straight. There has never been a foreign war on American soil. Do you hear me? Nuclear war *cannot happen* here." His voice is hard. "And I never want to hear about this again."

I stare at him, my mouth open, as an invisible wall bricks itself upward between us.

Another day, when we enter the house together, I walk ahead of him up the stairs. His voice floats up.

"You know, honey, you're looking really good lately." I vomit four times a day now. When we order pizza delivered to the house, I eat only the toppings off my single slice and throw away the bread, which annoys him. I lift weights. I drink bottle after bottle of Tab for the energy.

"You know," he says. "Slender." His voice is neutral, pleasant, as when ranking women at the mall. Like them, his voice suggests, I should be grateful. And I am: I rank. My father thinks I'm pretty.

I don't think of him below me on the stairs, looking up, evaluating my ass, my legs, my waist. There is no connection between this moment and my stepfather circling me in the forest, his Nikon clicking and whirring. My beloved, distant father thinks I'm pretty, and that's all that matters.

*   *   *

When I'm twenty-nine, my father and his wife drive from West Virginia for the day to see me in D.C., where I'm interviewing for positions with colleges and universities at the Modern Language Association convention: twelve thousand festive believers assembled together in a city, sitting still for one lecture after another.

It's my last day; my interviews are over — the lovely one, the all-right ones, the dreadful one. My father and his wife come to my hotel room, which I'm sharing with the woman with the edgy prison dissertation. She still has a few interviews to go and is getting ready, curling her hair. They all smile and chat while I get my coat and wallet.

We eat Chinese food together and talk, walk the town, go to the National Museum of Women in the Arts. For a couple of years, I've been fascinated by an Italian painter, a woman who took her rapist to court and endured torture — the way witnesses' veracity was proved then — to convict him, and who went on to paint biblical scenes of revenge: Judith and Holofernes, and so on. I'm as interested in the life as in the work, a vulgar tendency against which graduate study has schooled me but which I cannot seem to help.

In the museum store, we find a book about her. My father flips through it. He stops at her self-portrait: her round cheeks, dark eyes alert and smart, her arm upraised with the brush.

"Honey," says my father, "you know, this painter looks a lot like your friend. Don't you think?"

I look at the painting for a moment, and then at my father. I've known my friend for four years, have sat across her kitchen table from her, laughing. There is no resemblance. Then it occurs to me. My friend's a little overweight, something that bothers her, that she gripes about. Gentileschi was, by modern standards, plump. The arm lifting the brush is rich, fleshy.

My father looks at me, expectant, proud to have noted the one thing that matters. He has classified, compared. He has not seen their faces.

"Don't you think so, honey?" he says insistently. I don't know where to begin.

"I don't see it," I say, unwilling to ruin our day together.

"Oh." He puts the book down, piqued.

When I'm fifteen, a show comes on TV about a girl who dies from anorexia. One evening, when my stepmother's out somewhere and Tony's asleep, my father and I are sitting on stools in the kitchen, relaxed and easy. I tell him about the vomiting — that I want to see someone, get help. He stares at me for a long minute. Only the incandescent light over the sink is on; the dining room and living room have fallen away into darkness.

Finally, he stands and speaks in his bland, rational voice, the beautiful voice that is hired for spots on local radio and voice-overs on TV commercials. "That's the most disgusting thing I've ever heard," he says. He draws away from me, refills his coffee cup, tears open two pink Sweet'N Lows and pours them in. He looks at me. "That's disgusting." I feel a horrible sinking inside my limbs; *disgusting* is my mother's word for me, not my father's. "I'll tell you what's going to happen," he says. "You stop this nonsense — by yourself — by the end of the month, or I'll send you to an institution where they'll stop it for you." One of the majorettes who threw up to make weight, a girl in my class, was sent to a place in Ohio and has not come back.

I ask him not to. He shakes his head, sips his coffee. His voice is hard, like when he talks about an employee he's had to fire. "Well, you fix it, then."

My voice collapses, for the first and only time, into its old British accent, the voice of early childhood, of learning to talk, of first form. My father snorts, jerks like a startled horse. "Stop it," he says. "You sound ridiculous."

"I'm sorry," I say. "I'm sorry." I can't control it. I'm ashamed. All through the two years with my stepfather, this never happened. "I can't help it," I say. He squints at me, his mouth a smirk of disgust. Tears run down my face. "You think I'm pretending, don't you? Or crazy," I sob.

His nod is quick and sure. "Yes, I do. One or the other." He pulls away from my outstretched hands. But my words keep lurching out in their arched vowels, crisp consonants. I am mad. We both know it. The room is quaking, vibrating, everything a weird shade of yellow. My eyeballs are electric. He leaves, and I stand there, gripping the Formica. Down the hall, his door shuts.

Within the month, I stop vomiting. I just cease to do it. I inform him.

"Good," he says, and we don't mention it again.

Lonely, afraid of myself, my strangeness, I begin to wonder about my birth mother. Spanish is my only link to her. All I know is that she is Latina, maybe Cuban.

I learn in school the language my father will not speak at home. In college I will study the likeliest cultures (Cuban, Dominican, Mexican, Puerto Rican) and write poems that riff pretentiously on the notion of the mother tongue, inventing her girlhood in Miami, the Catholic high school, the handsome boyfriend forbidden by her parents, the tryst of my conception. I write it like a call sent out to her, imagining for myself a prehistory, a culture.

As a doctoral student, I will take one of my foreign-language exams in Spanish. I read everything by the cadre of Latina writers beginning to emerge. I want to be ready.

My mother's letters continue to arrive, criticizing my father's love of material things, which Witnesses must despise, and accusing us of living there for the same reason, a worldly love of luxury. But Tony and I are more ambivalent than she guesses.

On the living room wall hangs my father's favorite saying, cross-stitched by his wife: *He who dies with the most toys wins.*

"He who dies with the most toys still dies," we say to each other, when he's not there.

"Of course we're selfish," my father and his wife like to say. "Selfishness is healthy." On their bedroom wall is a large poster, a close-up of a woman's browned belly, ringed with a chain of shark's teeth, the Caribbean a turquoise line in the background. *HEDO-NISM*, the large white letters read.

In some ways, it is a welcome relief from the denial and asceticism of our mother's house. But there are no trust funds, no savings accounts for my brother and me. Our father doesn't forbid college; he just believes it's unnecessary, something for rich people's kids. If he got along without it, anyone can, as long as they're smart and work hard.

"It's a different world now," I say. "People need college if they want to get a good job."

"The world is the world. Cream rises."

For my allowance, I do everyone's laundry, empty and load the dishwasher, and mow the lawn each week. It seems so light, so easy, nothing. And I get money for it, money for college.

As a high school senior, I've finished most of my credits, so I get a full-time job. I leave school at noon and work until 9 P.M. at a factory, manufacturing artificial hip joints out of titanium.

My only criteria for college are that it be paid for and far away, someplace where it doesn't snow. A good private university offers a full academic scholarship. At sixteen, I arrive on a campus in Texas and find the kind of world I'd dreamed about. Ideas. Literature. Friends.

But I learn, too, that parents have saved for years to send their children there — that to do so is a middle-class assumption. I meet few working-class kids, but their parents, too, have saved for years, have gone without for their kids' sake. It's an aspect of parenthood I've never seen before. My grades dip.

At seventeen, when tuition is hiked during my second year, I drop out. I rent a one-room cottage with my bass-playing boyfriend and wait tables. My father signs the papers that declare me an independent minor, so I can get loans to go back. Working part-time as a security guard, part-time as a waitress, I hang out with kids who drive their parents' hand-me-down Volvos, who ski at Vail over spring break, who can afford to study abroad.

After my brother and I have moved out of the house, my father and his wife buy a boat, rare cameras, an RV, a van, an SUV, a model train that sits abandoned in their basement after a few months, new furniture, a cabin in Pennsylvania.

They live for each other, my father says, and that's what they spend their money on: their own pleasure.

When my brother graduates, they present him with an eight-page legally binding document that describes the conditions he'll have to meet if they're to contribute, even partially, to his education at the state university nearby.

He won't sign. "Fuck your contract." He moves into a mobile home with some friends, puts himself through school, drops out after a year. He becomes a mechanic, a good one.

In time, he moves to Austin, buys a house, breaks soil for a garden, brews beer, boats on the lake, learns to cook paella. He makes a wide circle of friends — bookstore managers, teachers, social workers, biologists, engineers — who laugh easily, celebrate holidays together, and adore him: his steadiness, his quick wit, his kindness. He reads books, argues politics, falls in love.

But he'd wanted to be an engineer.

16

When I'm a junior in college, I telephone my stepmother. Grey is sleeping in the middle of my bed, and I'm on the floor with my back to the wall.

"I just wanted to thank you," I say. I've been thinking about it for a while, and I can hear the gratitude, ungainly, surging in my voice. "To really thank you."

"For what?"

"It's about Grey." It's hard to start. "You know, my mom, she didn't really know how— I mean, she loved us, but— And Dad's great. You know that. But he's not always the most sensitive . . ." It's harder to say than I'd thought it would be, but it seems important to get out. "Anyway, you were so kind to us, so gentle." Her silence makes me nervous.

I don't say that I'm taking five courses, or that the dean would give me only two weeks off for childbirth, or that I can't afford a fifty-cent soft drink between classes. I don't talk about what it was like to have been the only pregnant student I'd ever seen on our country-club campus, ragged in my Goodwill clothes and hand-done haircuts against its smooth lawns and pretty brick buildings, or

192

about taking the bus downtown once a month to hear lectures about the basic food groups so I can get the WIC cards for our orange juice and milk, or about being afraid at night in the run-down neighborhood where we live, where arson, violence, and drug deals are public and routine. About how most of my college friends suddenly have better things to do, but how it doesn't matter.

I don't say that from the moment I knew Grey was growing, I abandoned all the illicit habits that had left me aimless and lost. That I took the steps no one showed me how to take, that I couldn't have been bothered to take on my own behalf. That while pregnant I ate nutritious food like my life depended on it — because his did. That I'd taken child psychology, to understand what he would need. That the slow changes of pregnancy, the overwhelming hours of natural childbirth, and now the simple daily tasks of care for someone innocent had shifted the pieces in my head, made me feel purposeful, capable, necessary for the first time, effecting a strange and unpredicted transformation. Or that I'd gone, trembling, to the university's free counseling center, determined to become what I never had. I don't tell her about nursing while reading *Bleak House,* or how Grey sleeps in my lap like a sacred trust while I type papers, or how I look down at him, into the face of peace, amazed, thinking, *He is the happy accident of my life.*

I can't put into words an equally strange thing: the way a slip-knot between my brows has come undone, and how I focus on that spot, eyes closed, for the brief breaks between tasks, falling into a dark grace where words and thoughts cease. Like prayer without praying. I get up with a calm energy new to me.

I don't tell her that my professor said I should consider graduate school (and I said, "What's graduate school?" and she told me) or that I'm finishing the semester with a healthy baby and straight A's. I don't utter the powerful new thought that's pulsing through me: *If I can do this, I can do anything.*

Instead I focus on her, so she'll listen. Gratitude is the feeling I'm having, like I've awakened into a clean world, and I want to thank everyone there is to thank.

"What I mean is, now that I have a baby, it's easy to be gentle with him," I say. "I can hold him, pat him, stroke his hair. I know how. I mean, it seems like the most natural thing in the world. I never feel like shaking him, or hitting, or talking in a mean way, or any of the stuff our mom did." He rolls a little on the bed, and I lower my voice. "He's just — so amazing, so little and soft . . . I mean, it seems crazy to even imagine that someone could want to hurt him. Sometimes my mom was gentle, but other times— And without you, the way you treated us, gentle all the time, I might not have known how to do it. I mean, I felt that way when Tony was little, too, but still, I just wanted to thank you. You always treated us so well."

She's silent.

"So anyway, like I said, I wanted to thank you."

There's a long pause. I slide the phone cord back and forth across my bare toes. Finally, she speaks.

"I don't know how to put this," she says. "But you need to know that I didn't do it for you." She sighs. Her tone is tired. "Look, it was all for your father. I would have done anything for him. I loved him so much. Do love him." She pauses again. "I'm just trying to be honest here, to be really clear with you."

"Thanks," I say.

"You know I wasn't crazy about having you two move in with us. Why would I be?"

"Sure," I say. I clear my throat. "You were young."

"Exactly. I mean, I never signed on for that. I was in my early twenties — just a little older than you are now. I'm sure you can understand how it was. I mean, we were in love."

"Right."

"Two kids? Come on. I never wanted to be a mother, even a stepmother, really. My own parents were so — well, I never wanted kids of my own. Still don't. Your father and I, we were having a romance. The time of our lives. A weekend or two a month was plenty."

"Okay," I say.

"But your father wanted you, and the situation you were in with your mother was just so awful. How could anyone say no?"

"Sure." I think back to that house, its ethic. No pets: they'd be a nuisance if we traveled. No houseplants. No plantings in the yard; the flowerbox sat empty, a span of bare dirt, until I planted seeds. When I called from a pay phone to say I was pregnant, no one said, "You can come home if you need to." I suddenly see that I've misunderstood.

"I just want to be clear that it wasn't for you, wasn't about you. So there's no confusion later on. Okay?"

"Okay."

"If I seemed kind, I was just doing what came naturally. And if I tried any extra, I was doing it for your father."

"Okay."

"I mean, you were great kids and all. Don't get me wrong. I couldn't have asked for better kids. Polite, smart. But I just want to be clear. There wasn't anything personal about it, between you and me, I mean, or between me and Tony. It was all for Lee."

Afterward, I sit in the little room for a long time, listening to the baby's breathing and the wind moving through the leaves.

A couple of years later, living with Grey in two seedy rooms, without a car or a friend in the new town where we've moved so I can start graduate school, I begin to look for my biological mother in earnest.

At twenty-three, working on a master's, I publish my first story, a queer, elliptical thing that never states directly its central event. No one in the workshop understands or likes it, except the professor. He publishes an article about its experimental form.

Later, I will publish more stories, and other scholars will write about them. But nothing will ever feel quite like that first one, which came as if by dictation: a daughter's elegy for her father, dead by suicide.

Hypersensitive.

At a department picnic, as I follow Grey, toddling around after the ducks, a friend introduces me to another graduate student. She thinks we'll like each other, and we do. He wanders along with us, content with our erratic, duck-led path.

I slowly become friends with him, a quiet, kind-eyed man, quick with a quip but gentle, an athlete who studies Chaucer, takes in stray animals, contains multitudes — a patient man, who always has a smile for Grey and can play endlessly with Legos. Who grew up sailing with his dachshund on Lake Pontchartrain, camping in bayous with friends, and wishing his stable family would talk a little more. One day, after two years of comfortable friendship, I notice, with a start, that he is handsome.

We're both grad-school broke: on our first date, he cooks for me — pasta, asparagus, mushrooms, artichoke hearts, and pesto. After dinner, he rubs my feet. He asks questions, likes to listen. He has no expectations.

A few years later, we marry.

When I am twenty-six, working on a doctorate, I find my mother, Sharon, the orange-haired woman with owl glasses. For years her information has been in the databank of the international adoption registry in Nevada, waiting for someone to match the date and hospital with mine.

When I get the call and hear her voice, when I put my suitcase down on her floor, everything comes shifting and unsettled in my heart. She is a feminist, an educator, a graceful woman with large dark eyes and a kind smile.

Bread pudding, my favorite dessert, is her favorite. She has raised her two children gently, without spanking or sarcasm. She has no religion. "I feel God all the time," she says. I cannot stop looking at her hands.

I am not Cuban, I learn — not Latina at all. The attorney lied to my parents to speed up the adoption. I am French, Irish, Cherokee, she tells me; my grandmother's people live in Oklahoma, where the Trail of Tears ended. That's where the coloring comes from, why people always said I was the spitting image of my father.

When I think of all the Spanish courses I've taken in high school and college, the doctoral exam in Spanish, all the Latina literature I've devoured to be ready to commune with her — all the attempts to recover what my father's efforts at assimilation hid, thinking it was mine to find — I laugh, because laughing is the only thing to do. I discovered a beautiful world: not mine, but beautiful.

I was conceived, she tells me, in romance. She was twenty, and he was the first man she'd slept with, and they were in love. They left the theater in the middle of *Doctor Zhivago* to rush back to his apartment.

Her mother sent her from the Midwest to Miami, pregnant, and threw away each letter he sent. Not until years later would she learn he'd written. Her mother finally told her — when she was married to another man, when it was too late to look.

After she'd gotten over the panic, she says — the initial panic of being pregnant and twenty and single — she'd wanted me. She wanted me now.

I lie on the grass in the backyard, staring up through branches at the hot blue Texas sky, trying to feel my way into what it all means.

17

For several years, when I talk on the phone with my father — during college, grad school, the first years of teaching — I describe my recent small achievements, and he says how proud he is. Together with the movies, it's our only currency. If I've achieved nothing, his voice grows bored. But the conversations I have with my father during the last couple years of his life — those years, our stepmother tells us later, when she began to see signs of depression — follow a strange pattern of denial and recovery.

My father is a man severed from himself, a man of self-evasions.

"You know something?" he says one day, out of the blue. He has come to visit us in Indiana, where I've taken the job. He's driving; Grey and I are in his red Chevy Blazer. From his rearview mirror hangs a small sculpture of polished crystal, a tiny transparent cock and balls. As we drive, it swings back and forth, casting rainbows across the upholstery. "I've never been attracted to Cuban women," he continues. "I just do not find them attractive." His tone is proud, as if he's just discovered this fascinating fact about himself.

I don't know how many ways that's inappropriate, I think. His eight-year-old grandson is looking at him with interest. I've learned already that I'm not Cuban, but I think of what a blow it would have otherwise been, to hear my father, oblivious to anyone's feelings but his own, say that me and my kind are just not attractive. I wonder how his sisters would feel, hearing him. Not to mention his dismissal of a whole group, as if all Cuban women look alike. But then it occurs to me.

"What about Sonia?"

His whole body shifts back a little, as if he's been gently struck.

"Right," he says slowly. "Sonia." The SUV decelerates. "Yes, that's right. I was attracted to Sonia." We pass a cornfield and the grocery store. "Funny, how I thought of that without ever remembering her. I was completely sure — when I said it — that I'd never been attracted to a Cuban girl in my life." He explains to Grey that Sonia was the girl he loved in high school, a beautiful girl whose arm was withered from polio and whom he had once, long ago, hoped to marry.

I cannot imagine this: her polio, her less-than-perfect arm, for my father cannot bear imperfection of any sort. If a child on the street has some visible handicap, he averts his eyes. He finds it too painful, he says; he would rather not see them. When we converse, he refuses to discuss problems of any sort, or even to listen to them. If I can't think of some small new achievement to describe when I call each Sunday, we talk about movies or the weather. When my stepmother begins to see a counselor, after I've gone away to college, and comes home crying, he makes her choose: therapy or him. He doesn't want to deal with her this way. She stops going, chooses him over herself, she whispers to me on the phone.

"Leave him," I say. "That's crazy. That's too much to ask."

"You don't understand. He's my whole life."

So his love for Sonia is strange to me. I cannot imagine how a boy so accepting of weakness could become the man I know.

*   *   *

Sonia, if you read this: my father never really stopped loving you. In the last years of his life, he carried your photograph. You and Key West were an island torn out of him, floating out of reach.

The rest of us were just what came after.

My father comes again to visit — my father and his beautiful voice, his endless stories of minutiae, starring himself. The deal he got on soda at Sam's Club. What he said to the guy at work. The laughing anecdotes about nothing that people will remember him for after he's dead. His ability to work a room.

"I've never met anyone who could turn getting a key made at the hardware store into a saga," my husband says.

"It's a gift," I agree.

My birth mother travels to our house to meet him. She calls later. "Now I see why you and your brother are so quiet," she says. "How could you have gotten a word in edgewise?"

I'm sitting on the couch one day, talking on the phone with him, two states away. We're talking about his efforts to write down his memories of childhood. He'd been thinking, he says, about things he hadn't thought of for fifty years.

He tells me his earliest memory, the air raids in Key West when he was very small, too young to understand, everything plunging to blackness, the adults grabbing him and dragging him under the table, crying, never knowing if it was a practice run or if the Japanese had targeted the island's naval base.

"It was just terrifying," he says. His voice sounds strangely naked, unlike him. "I was terrified." He clears his throat. "And that's my earliest memory."

Sitting there, I feel a tremor run from my skull down to my spine, and raw data shakes suddenly into clarity. This is why he was so adamant about nuclear war, so blunt and impervious about it when I was in high school. He didn't want me to feel afraid, the way he had felt afraid. He was trying to save me from it. The denial was for me, his daughter. Strange gift. Something fights in my throat.

"You've never told me about that before."

His tone lightens. "Well, honey, I don't ever really think about it."

After his death, I tell my stepmother.

"Oh, no," she says. "He told me about the air raids. He said he loved them. That they were really exciting."

She says that his earliest memory was hiding under a table, scared, while his parents fought. He never mentioned this to my brother and me. He always described his home life as perfectly happy. "We weren't poor," he liked to say. And then, like a punch line: "We just never had any money." A characterization of them as relentlessly upbeat. And then he would tell some chipper anecdote.

My earliest memory. In the brick apartment house in Weybridge, I watch out the window, guarding the lawn. I am nearly three.

I have quickly learned the English views toward grass, having been pulled off it abruptly by my parents, having had strange men in uniforms approach and speak gruffly, pointing to little white signs.

The grass in front of our apartment, I have decided, is our grass. Our garden. I am sick of being scolded and plan to do some scolding of my own. A figure runs by in blue pants and a red sweater, and I run to the door. I open it and yell, "Boy! Boy! Don't step on our grass!"

My mother is suddenly there, grabbing my shoulders, shaking me, pulling me back into the house, and slamming the door. Her eyes are squinty with anger, but her eyebrows are afraid.

"Don't you ever do that!" she says. Her voice is a harsh whisper. "Do you hear me?"

I start to cry. "He was on our grass!"

"Don't you ever call a black man *boy*. Do you hear me? That's wicked. Wicked." She shakes me. "I don't ever want to hear you say that again. Do you understand?"

I nod, sniffling, trying to remember what part of him was colored black.

My father, who raised us to check the White box, to flatten the pronunciation of our surname, whose skin tanned to a deep brown and never burned, was secretly scared of darkness.

In Key West, Cuban was white, white enough, with all the rights and privileges thereof. Unless you were too dark.

After Catholic elementary school, a Filipino friend of his had been questioned by the public high school officials. Too dark, they thought; he'd have to go to the colored school. His parents protested at the office with his birth certificate, and he attended high school with my father.

"So what was it like for black people there?" I ask on the phone. I'm a new professor, teaching a course on race relations in the United States. Nanny, his mother, gave me the one black doll I had as a child, named Elizabeth for the street she lived on, Elizabeth like my middle name, a beautiful baby doll in a dress with tiny green and purple flowers.

"Oh, they had it very good," he says. "No prejudice. Everyone respected them. They had separate schools, but there was a lot of politeness. No violence, no tension, nothing like that."

"Well, that's good."

"In fact, sweetie," he says, his tone brightening, "they even had things we didn't. Yeah, that's right. You know, I remember being envious as a kid because they had their own swimming pool. Blacks only. Only pool on the island. All of us boys wanted to get in. But we weren't allowed. There was a really high fence around it." He thinks for a moment. "I remember my parents talking about it. All the black social groups and community clubs got together and raised the money for it."

A couple of seconds tick by.

"Why did they build a swimming pool?"

"What?"

"Why did they need to?"

"Why did they need to build a swimming pool?" he repeats. "Well, I don't know, but we sure did want to— Oh my God." His tone is different, the brightness gone. "Oh, Jesus, honey."

"What?"

"They built the pool," he says slowly, as if realizing it for the first time himself, "because they weren't allowed on the beaches." He clears his throat. "Well, there were these two beaches where they could swim, if they wanted. But they were rocky. No one wanted to swim there." He's quiet for a long moment. Key West is an island ringed by sand.

"Wow," I say.

"For fifty years, I haven't thought about that. Whenever I thought about race relations in Key West, I always remembered how civil it was, how decent, compared to the rest of the country, how crazy it all got then, riots, violence." He sighs. "I always remembered that damn swimming pool, and how my friends and I wanted to get in there." His voice is sad and full. "Jesus, honey," he says. "They couldn't even take their kids to the beach. In Key West. They couldn't take their kids to the beach." This seems to be what bothers him most, a man who loved to take us places, who loved teaching us to swim.

I send him the book on race I've been using in the course. He loves it. He calls to tell me how excited he is. All his life, he says, he's seen the things the author writes about, but he's never added it all up the way she does. On the phone, he makes me wait while he gets the book to read me lines he's marked.

After he dies, it's on his reading table in the living room, next to the recliner. I open it to see which pages he has dog-eared. "Familism," is a heading he's underlined in the chapter on Latinos: the way Hispanic people tend to prize family connections above material wealth or other cultural values. "Speaking Spanish," about the way Latinos preserve the language, cultivating it in their children as the most profound and visible marker of identity.

There's a gap between what my father knows, and what he knows he knows.

There's a reason he stopped speaking Spanish, stopped admiring the beauty of Cuban women, but I have to run a man down in the street to learn it.

I'm thirty-one and on my way to the office on a bright day in June. It's the noon hour, and the streets of the little town are crowded. I'm doing twenty-five past the courthouse when a man in green jogging shorts and a brown ponytail darts full-speed in front of my car. He hits, rolls upward onto the windshield, and falls.

I brake and get out in the middle of traffic, not knowing I'm covered with fragments of glass. Medics rush past — an ambulance had happened to be three cars back — and I stand by my open door repeating, "No," as his bloody body twists on the asphalt.

They crouch over him, lift him onto a stretcher to carry him away. A woman's hand is squeezing my hand, brushing the glass away from my eyes. Her voice says,

"What is your name? Can you tell me your name?"

I stammer it.

"What's your address?" She stays with me until more medics arrive and put me in another ambulance to make sure I'm not in shock.

A police officer drives me home; my car is towed away. I spend the afternoon wandering dazed around the house. I call the hospital, send flowers, forget to eat and bathe. Eyewitnesses tell the police there was no way I could have stopped. When I go to the garage the next day, still in a stupor, to see about the car, a switch of brown hair juts from the shattered windshield, and I retch onto the gravel.

By the time I call my father some days later, I'm all right, and the man is out of danger. My father says how sorry he is about it all. And then, in his most firm and definite tone, as though he's just closed a highly beneficial but still unimpeachably legal deal, he says, "Nothing like that has ever happened to me." He says it with what sounds like pride.

"Okay," I say, a little bewildered. It doesn't seem like the most sympathetic thing to say in the circumstances.

"Never," he says.

"Okay." One of those weird Dad-centric comments, I think.

There's a long, strange pause.

"Wait a minute," he says. His tone is round and shocked. "Something *did* happen to me once, something like that."

"What?"

"I can't believe it. I haven't thought about it in years." He tells me the story.

Long before my father is my father, he is a boy of eighteen, ambitious and in love with a beautiful Cuban-American girl named Sonia. When he moves from Key West to Miami, he lives with Sonia's mother, who has a house there. He gets work driving a truck — good enough for the moment. He'll earn enough to send for Sonia, and they'll marry.

He's driving his own car; he's at a busy intersection, about to make a left. His signal's blinking, and he could make it, but a police motorcycle is gunning fast toward him, so he waits. But the officer doesn't think he's going to wait. He lays the cycle down on its side as he brakes and loses control, and his body flings onto the windshield of my father's car. He lies sprawled on the pavement.

My father gets out, horrified, shocked, bewildered. In a minute, six squad cars are there. Police surround him, their guns drawn and pointed at his head. The ambulance comes as he's thrown, speechless, against his car. They cuff him, inspect the contents of his wallet, and throw him into the back of a squad car. His body shakes. He stares out the window, trying to see what's going on. No one speaks to him on the drive to the station.

Much later, when he's released, he will go, scared and sad, to the hospital and apologize to the officer, who will say not to worry, it was his own damn fault. Despite this, for two years, my father will go only to work, to obtain food, and to his domicile, as the court has ordered, until the case is cleared up. The police stop him any-time they want. If he's not on his way to or from work or food, he can be jailed. For two years, he obeys, and then he is cleared of all charges.

Trembling in the backseat of a cop car, he knows none of this. He knows only the awful bleeding of a strange man on a bright street, the smack of his own breastbone against metal, the quick snatch of his wallet, which flaps open in the hand of a cop who walks away, leans into the dark cavern of a car, and talks into his other hand.

They drive. They say nothing. Not knowing what to do, not wanting to be rude, and still shaking with shock, he does not address them. At the station, they hustle him through to a cell and slam him inside. They're walking away.

"Wait!" cries the eighteen-year-old suddenly, panicked beyond protocol. "What's going to happen now?" One officer turns back, surprised, his eyebrows rising up behind his sandy bangs.

"For Christ's sake, boy, we didn't know you spoke English."

"I speak English. I speak English."

"The name on your license, boy. We called for a translator already. We're waiting for him now." The cop's surprised look fades and tightens. A man is down and might be dying. He turns to walk away.

"But what's going to happen to me?" my father calls.

The officer spins, angry now. "What happens? He dies, boy, and you'll get the chair."

The shudders that will sweep in waves over the eighteen-year-old have not begun when the cop disappears down the hallway, mut-tering racist imprecations, which my father will not repeat on the phone decades later, as the barred door clangs shut.

After my father dies, I ask my stepmother if I can have a copy of the memoir he's been working on for the past couple of years, since I sent him a piece I published about his childhood in Key West, and he began to write.

"What memoir?" she says. She is certain he had never mentioned one.

"Just search for it, please. On his computer."

She can't find anything labeled *memoir,* or anything similar, she will tell me later on the phone, after we've driven back to our own lives.

"Try looking for the keyword *poinciana,*" I say, a tree that had been in his yard on Elizabeth Street when he was a boy and was there no longer, a tree I'd never seen, a tree he'd spoken about with longing when he'd told me he was starting to write, starting to try to recall his life.

The document came up immediately, she says, her voice surprised. Later, she mails me the pages: a meticulous, clear, closely detailed rendering of anecdotes from his early years. Emotionless, in flawless English.

Though the civil rights era is over by the time I am born, my parents were both young adults when it unfolded. They never spoke of it — I didn't hear the phrase until college — but I think it did affect them: my father tried very hard to be white, and my mother, who was white, tried very hard to be nice to people who weren't.

I fill in what my father, telling me about the accident with the police, does not articulate. During those two years of limbo, he breaks it off with Sonia. He stops speaking Spanish, except to his parents on the phone. He will never be attracted to another Cuban woman. He will bury Sonia and Spanish so deep he has to be reminded they exist. Only from the safe distance of his fifties and sixties will he speak of them again.

After those two years, my father dated and married only white women: my mother, English-Irish-Hungarian, her pale skin freckling with too much sun. The random women we met and never saw again. Our willowy stepmother, luminous, blue-eyed, blond.

My mother, in her own way and for reasons I can't know, chose only Latin men. My father was Spanish and Cuban; my stepfather's heritage is Italian, as is her third husband's. She fetishized black people, too, but as the friends whose company she especially sought or as some convenient version of The Folk, simple and dear and needy, to give rides to the Kingdom Hall to, but not to marry.

Both my parents mistrusted and abstained from politics, joining instead — my father briefly, my mother for life — a religion that recognized all people as equals, that had seen the world that way even in the 1920s and '30s, when most of America hadn't: the kitschy, well-meaning illustrations on the endpapers of Watchtower books from the Jazz Age and Depression: a Mexican family all in sombreros, an African family in embroidered A-line robes, a clean-cut white family, a Chinese family in their conical straw hats, all of the families standing together, their faces raised toward heaven, where a pale, bearded Jesus rides down on a horse.

18

After my father dies, I read books about suicide — like numbed Krebs in Hemingway's *In Our Time*, reading books about the war he's just fought to get a sense of perspective, of what the purpose and plan of it all had been, which, on the ground, he hadn't been able to see.

I learn that people, before killing themselves, often attempt to make amends with their loved ones. I do not know this when, one month before he takes his life, my father starts to call me every day.

He is distraught; our stepmother has left him. He is broken-hearted. Everything she wanted him to do, he did: live separately, make other friends, spend only a little time together. But now she wants a divorce as well, and doesn't want his last name anymore. Still she comes to the house to make love; still she says she loves him. He cannot comprehend it. Is the lovemaking a lie? Why does she see her therapist outside the office? Is she having an affair?

My stepmother doesn't return my calls, my e-mails. I leave messages saying that I understand her leaving, that I love her, that I know how tyrannical my father and his opacity, his edicts, can be. But she doesn't get in touch. It's hard to know what to think. His walls are gone.

He calls two or three times a day, sometimes for an hour at a time. Sometimes, he cries. Sometimes, we just talk. I have the chance to tell him how much I love him, how much Grey and I need him. He is sad, but he is open, all at once — the father I'd always wanted, could remember from before he'd remarried, had always known was there, under the mask of professional cool.

"I can't believe how selfish I've been," he says once. "Putting all my eggs in one basket, emotionally." His voice catches. "I can't believe what I've missed all these years, barely knowing you kids. Oh, God, honey," he says. "I'm so sorry. I've been so selfish."

The words are magical, like a balm. It's all right, I tell him. None of it matters now. What matters is the future.

The eight-page document, he says, the one about my brother's college, is what he regrets most. Our stepmother wrote it. "I didn't know anything about college," he said. "I thought she knew what to do. I just let her do it. I feel like I betrayed my son." Tell him, I say.

I have to give a paper at a literary conference in Long Beach, but he calls my hotel every evening, and we talk late into the night.

"You were only gone four days," my husband says when I return. "Can't he give you a break?"

His remark surprises me; he's right. But it hasn't occurred to me to want a break. My father, after years of managerial distance, is talking to me like a real person. We're mending all the bridges I'd given up trying to cross. We're finally going to have the connection I've longed for.

"Do you think he was just giving us what he thought we wanted?" my brother asks afterward. "You always wanted him to be honest; I just wanted him to be a buddy." Our father had called him, too, that last month, but they had discussed light, cheerful things, Tony says: what's going on, this and that. Guy stuff, he says.

Several times, we each had offered to come stay with him, see him through it, bring him back to stay with us, but he'd fobbed us off. His good friends Larry and Ricardo, he said, were making sure he had plenty of fun things to do, his therapist was looking out for him, and as soon as he'd gotten this divorce thing squared away, he'd be out to see us. He was doing fine. Difficult, but fine.

With no evidence to the contrary from his wife, we let ourselves be reassured. Tony and I welcomed the phone calls, the closeness, the father we'd wanted. Each of us thought a new era had begun. Ice to the Eskimos.

Father's Day weekend, 2002. On Saturday, I wake up late and am drinking iced coffee on the back steps in the sun with my husband. Lazy, happy. I have an article to finish by Monday, but for right now, we have a little time just to sit.

I'm suddenly struck: if I jumped in the car now, I could be at my father's house by seven or so that evening. It's an eight-hour drive, depending on construction. I could spend Father's Day with him, a surprise, and be back in time for work Monday morning.

I call him. He's gotten the book, the box of Godiva chocolates, and the two cards — two, because I couldn't decide between the funny one and the tender one. Actually, he says, he has plans for to-morrow with his friend Larry. Besides, he's definitely going to come see us, just as soon as he returns his response to the divorce papers. Spend some real time with us, with Grey, no rushing.

If I had gone, I would have seen the new thinness, the dullness in his eye, the messy house, all the things my stepmother would later say had marked him, even physically, as depressed. Would have learned, perhaps, that his therapist wasn't his at all, was only my stepmother's, just talking to my father — who, ashamed of weak-ness, still leery of counselors, refused to seek help on his own — as a kindness, for free.

I could have taken him home with me, wouldn't have left without him. Would not have stopped until he got what he needed, whatever that was: a hospital stay, or medication, or a therapist concerned with only him. I could not have left him in that place alone. I would not have given up.

But I do not go. I stay and finish my article. It is the rational, professional thing to do. I am the adult he raised me to be.

Two weeks later, he's dead.

The week before my father dies, he tells me on the phone that I'm the only person in his life from whom he has ever felt unconditional love.

"The only one," he repeats. "I said that to a friend of mine the other day, in fact," he says, as if that authenticates it.

"Tony loves you like that, too."

"I know, I know," he says. "But you're the only one I ever *felt* it from."

In the dreams that come after my father's death, I am a bride in black lace, black thigh-high stockings, and my father is alive and I urge him, his face in my hands: "There is medication." I throw my arms around him and say, "You can make it through this. We love you, Grey loves you. We need you. There will be other women."

My stepmother suddenly exists. She grabs my shoulders and spins me around to face her, shaking me.

"You're nothing but a rare ambitious little bitch," she yells.

I want to yell back but don't know what to say. She may be right. I feel the weak fall of my rebuttal, its inadequacy, even as I'm saying it: "Well, you're a narcissistic person." Even my tone lacks anger.

I'm not being fair. After he handed her the suicide note in her office — as she stood there reading it — my father pulled out a gun and waved it at her. He looked unsure, she'd said. When she screamed and scrambled under a table, a colleague came in and got the gun away from him. He left and bought another without difficulty; his record was clean.

She's gone through enough. *Narcissistic.* My dream words fall weakly in the air.

She looks back at me, unfazed, pink Fiestaware blowing and rippling on the shelves around us.

In dream after dream, Dad, you are still alive, and I do everything I would have done if I had known how bad it was for you. Again and again, you are alive, I can still try, it's not too late.

After my father dies, during those days we spend in his house, I find in his filing cabinet a card that I made at five or six. For nearly thirty years, he saved it. It's made of memo paper from the airline in England, aged now as though soaked in tea. The brown broken stems of three flowers, their blossoms long snapped away, are taped inside.

"Daddy come home," it says on the front in bright crayon. A little girl with dark hair smiles.

Inside the girl eats her breakfast in the first frame, goes to school in the second, and comes home to be tucked into bed by her mother in a third. It was an hour's drive home from Heathrow; my father often arrived late at night. "Daddy come home" is printed under each. "Daddy come home." "Daddy come home."

In the final frame, her father, in a business suit, stands at last before her. But she has fallen asleep. "Oh, no!" the caption reads. Crayoned hearts float in the air between them.

Always, it seems, I was afraid of missing his return.

Now there is nothing left to fear. *Oh, no.*

When my father died, they took his eyes.

At her new house before the funeral, our stepmother keeps talking about the comfort we should take in that: the fact that he has given someone the gift of sight, that his death has not been entirely a waste. Later she mails us books about the loving act of organ donation.

His eyes. I'm afraid one day I'll see them, looking out at me from the face of a stranger. And I'll lose my mind.

19

I need to find some kind of closure, to move things into the past tense. To stop living them, and start putting them away. To impose some kind of order.

I have some hypotheses about my father's death.

Hypothesis I: The medicalization of sadness. My stepmother claims that he was clinically depressed, had been for the last couple of years. He would not seek help, would not consider medication. This refusal corresponds with the dad I knew.

But this matter of family members diagnosing one another is a tricky one; anyone who knows a few therapeutic terms from a magazine article can label someone sick. I've seen families use it as a handy way of dismissing a troublesome member.

We didn't know she believed he was ill. She didn't communicate with us during that time, and our phone calls and visits with him were the same. She says of course; he would never show weakness in front of his children. This rings true.

When they came to my house for Thanksgiving, that last fall before he died, they came as a couple, though they'd already been living separately for months. They mentioned nothing, gave nothing away. He couldn't bear for us to know, she said later, so she went along with the charade. I replayed the weekend in my mind again and again, but my father had been slick, bright, empty, talkative, the same as always.

Hypothesis II: The life-events explanation.

A. She was leaving him.

Ever since they married, all his pleasure, all his love — perhaps all his identity — had been bound up in her. In recent years, all he'd talked about was what they'd do together once he retired.

"I didn't want to be married to someone *old*," she told us after the funeral. "And your father was starting to act old, not like the young, fun-loving guy he'd always been." Her voice lowered. "You know, he told me once that what made him happiest in the world was to sit on the couch with me and watch TV. He was totally content. That was his idea of perfect happiness." She shook her head. "I didn't want to sit on the couch and watch TV." He still traveled — still drove on a whim to Manhattan to see *The Producers* with a friend. But he was slowing down. He didn't take her to Saint Thomas anymore.

I do not know why, when she was twenty-two or thirty-two, my stepmother failed to compute the future. I just know that, in her middle forties, the equation didn't look good.

So: he could not bear the thought of loneliness, or the pain of rejection, or the confusion: why was she divorcing him, if she still wanted to see him, have sex with him? She was making love with him just days before he died. Why was she seeing their therapist socially, outside of the office? Who was lying, and what was the truth?

Also, perhaps, he could not bear the humiliation. For years, people had praised and envied their marriage. They were the happiest married couple people had ever seen. Adoring, devoted, absorbed in each other. We heard it all the time, living there, and it was a mythology he loved and perpetuated.

Blind, self-absorbed, careless, yes, from my frustrated child's-eye point of view. But absolutely, undeniably happy, completely wrapped up in each other. Never an unkind word. Affectionate, romantic, and so on.

And now to be severed?

B. Retiring itself.

I think it is not an exaggeration to claim that my father lived (except for his wife) for work, to be praised at work, to be effective, to make his colleagues laugh, to be liked in the hangar by mechanics and by the higher-ups at dinner parties. He loved work. *"He was such an up person. He always had a personality that was cutting up and making light of everything," said Harrison-Marion Regional Airport manager,* it said in one of the flurry of newspaper articles after his suicide. Men I'd known as boys in high school found me on the Internet and e-mailed to offer condolences, ask how I was doing, if I was married. *"When I used to work for him several years ago, he would always say, 'Damn it, I'm not going to work here unless it's fun.'"*

Now work was gone. And the one thing he'd been looking forward to, a late-life version of an extended honeymoon, was gone, too.

He had sacrificed his heritage, a certain and significant portion of himself, for success at work and the love of a beautiful woman. Pulling away both at once was like pulling out the dual keystones of his life.

Hypothesis III: "The ultimate chickenshit dance." That's what Cool Julie called it, even before she flew north with my brother. Suicide as the act of a selfish coward, of someone who would abandon everyone rather than grow. And that seems reasonable as well.

These three are the easy, obvious ones, the ones available to anyone who knew him, knew them. They make sense of the situation, and I believe they are true. Undoubtedly, they are the truth.

However.

In the courtroom, you have to swear to tell the truth, the whole truth, and nothing but the truth.

If they were all the same thing, there wouldn't be three phrases.

Hypothesis IV: The psychopolitical factor. (And this is only a factor to be added, not a comprehensive explanation — not something that, by itself, I believe, could have pushed my father to kill himself. But it could be enough to weaken a person, to shake someone's will to live.)

There will never be an attack on American soil, my father believed and asserted, squelching the helpless terror of his own wartime childhood, denying to his children that such things could ever occur. He lied to provide us a bearable future.

It is no coincidence, I think, that before a year had passed after the 9/11 attacks — on the economic, political, and military centers of the American Dream, for which he had sacrificed so much of himself — my father was dead.

Hypothesis V: Sometimes our lives can have a strange and perfect symmetry, stranger than the symmetries of art.

When my father was eighteen, he sat in his car, confused and afraid, for himself and for the uniformed authority who had thudded to the pavement, bleeding. Afraid of the lights and sirens, of the approaching blue men with their badges and nightsticks, their drawn revolvers.

I think that something happened in that car, in that frozen moment of fear and shock, in that moment when he was thrown against and into a police car, not spoken to, and in that moment in the jail, when he learned that his coloring and the name on his license made him less a person than he'd thought he was, less an American — when, innocent in a jail cell, he was threatened with legal death. I think an eighteen-year-old boy died in that car, the best, most vital part of him, the man he would have become, the man who spoke Spanish and loved Cuban girls, the man who was open and hopeful and whole. Libano. Over the next two years, my father relinquished himself, his past, his language, his accent, his childhood sweetheart, and the charms of her Latina sisters everywhere. To survive in the world he wanted to enter — had, unknowingly, entered — he executed the boy he had been. And he spent forty-four years in limbo, trying to run from it and then, too late, trying to make it right.

In the last years of his life, he had been reviving that boy: writing down his memories, acknowledging his terror of the air raids, making friends with two Spanish teachers, and becoming fascinated with the powerful, complicated, self-invented Eva Perón, translating *Evita* into Spanish for his own amusement. In the summers, he started pulling the blinds shut, the way his mother had in his childhood to keep out the blaring Caribbean sun — which my stepmother, left to her own devices, read as a sign only of depression, not of return. ("I'm a day-time person," she told Tony and me, after his death. "I need lots of light. Light. And your father wanted it dark all the time.") And he had become sad. More truthful, but sad. He had given up the boy he'd been, and there was sadness in examining that, along with rediscovery's delight. But he was becoming old, undesirably old.

When his working years were over, when his pretty wife left him, he drove his red Chevy Blazer and parked. In his car, surrounded by police, he asked my stepmother on the cell phone to call off the cops — they talked until the moment he pulled the trigger, her at the police station, frantic, desperate to keep him alive, identifying his locations to the police as he drove around looking for a quiet parking lot. She tried; orders were given; the police officers retreated to positions farther off, encircling the vehicle more loosely. *Castro said he would shoot himself if he saw police closing in,* said one article. A police official *said that Castro told* his wife, *"If I can't do it, they'll do it for me."*

And then, while my father and his wife talked further, the police drew in close again. This time, they would not stop coming toward the car. The newspaper photographs show them with their drawn handguns, pointing at the red Blazer, encircling it. Hoping, perhaps, to talk him out of it, take the gun away. But they came too close.

And then he executed himself for the final time.

*   *   *

When Paul was a child, he thought as a child, he ate as a child, he spoke as a child. But when he became a man, he put away childish things.

I sometimes wonder if that hasn't been the tragedy of Christendom.

20

For years, I had known that our father kept a file of the custody battle: every legal document, every communication from our mother and stepfather, his own notes on the situation. When I tore my mother's letter up, he whisked it away to be filed. One day, he says, we will sit down together and look through it all. When I am ready. But he dies first.

His will, as we have always been told it would, leaves everything to his wife. In her new house before the funeral, we ask if, under the circumstances — her divorce suit, his suicide — she intends to make provision for us, or for Grey, his only grandchild. But there will be no provision.

"Well, yes, I had thought about doing something," she says, casting her eyes about the little room under the eaves, where the documents are.

"What?" Tony asks.

"I'm not sure yet. It's going to take a while to sort things out." She waves her hand vaguely, as if to say that details can come later.

She hands us instead photocopies of his bitter, lucid suicide note, two typed and dated pages that reiterate, "So, take it all, the house, the vehicles, the cabin, the life insurance, everything. Go and enjoy the life you think you want. . . ."

Once we see his note, we accede without question. They have always impressed upon us that his life insurance, a hundred thousand dollars, will go to her, not us. None of it comes as a surprise.

It takes something out of me, though: knowing that, even at the last, even blaming her for his death, he wanted to give everything he had to her.

We drive out to Valley Falls, a state park where we used to go with our father and then, as teenagers, with our friends. We walk in a numb, stunned way over the rocks by the river. It's a beautiful day. The forest is huge and green and twined with paths. Grey, restless, keeps disappearing ahead of us, and then, rounding a bend, we see him in the distance, farther away each time, leaping over shining water.

Later, when we arrive back at the house, where we once lived as children, our stepmother's older sister is there, sitting outside against the wall alone, sweating and stormy-eyed, a bottle of water dangling between her spread knees. She's flown in from California, a fake blond with fake breasts and, usually, a fake smile, which now is gone.

"Can I talk to you two?" she says, her eyes full of a meaning I can't read. "Inside?"

"Sure," we say.

She rushes up the steps ahead of us, furious. She helps herself to our father's recliner, where she sits, going on and on, berating us for asking about the will at a time like this, for putting her sister through this.

"You know how you two feel about each other? Well, that's how I feel about her. She's my little sister. I'm going to protect her from any crap from the two of—"

"We wanted to know our father's last wishes," I say, slow with shock, lowering myself to the couch. Had our stepmother complained about us after we left? She must have. Well, it doesn't matter. "We have the right to know what his last wishes are," I say, but she doesn't stop speaking. Tony stays standing, his hands loose by his sides.

"—and she doesn't need the two of you coming in here, harassing her. It wasn't as if she was some kind of *fly-by-night* wife, you know. She's been a good, loyal wife for over twenty years, and your father wasn't exactly—"

"It was our right to know." I say it in a firm voice, more loudly. My hands are beginning to tremble.

"Well, you had no business—"

"You need to get out," Tony says quietly, suddenly. His hands, I notice, are closed now.

"What?" she cries, outraged, her voice veering upward into a shriek. "Are you *throwing* me out of this house? After all I've done? I helped *clean* this house when I got here. Your father left it a complete —"

"You just really need to leave now," my brother says, and his body inclines very slightly toward her.

Flustered, offended, muttering, she rises.

"I hope you feel righteous," I say as she heads out the door.

"Righteous? Jesus," she mutters in disgust. Then I feel silly, childish, for having said it.

Later, through both memorial services, she will act as if we are not there, as if my brother and I and the people we love do not exist.

When our stepmother returns to the house, I ask if I can have my father's blue sweatshirt that I used to borrow in high school — it was a game, each of us trying to get to the dryer first to grab it. I ask for the stupid china figurines he and our mother got a lifetime ago on vacation in Hawaii and gave to Nanny, who then left them to him when she died: a male and female dancer, shaking gourds, adorned with flowers, brown bodies in cream clothes. As a little girl, I stared at them on Nanny's mirrored shelves in Key West. Silly, worthless figurines, a man and a woman. All that's left.

Tony takes Nanny's china tigers, the rusting San Francisco street sign that says *Castro St.*, and Papi's old Mason stuff: a gavel, a mosaic. And Dad's Lions Club pins. The things that made them men in their communities.

I take a few old black-and-white photographs that have Dad and me in them, and my brother takes a few. I find six old Bobbsey Twins books in the basement and take those, too.

And the file, I say: I want the file.

"Sure," she says. "Help yourself. God, I don't want it."

When I sit down alone to read it, one month later, my stomach will bleed.

There has been a gap in this narrative, as there is in my memory.

I am in no position to condemn the processes of repression, evasion, denial. Sometimes they are how you survive.

For twenty years after that time in the trailer, when I thought back to it, I was ashamed. I could not see why I had flipped so quickly, why I had asked my father to seek custody but then done everything I could to thwart his suit. I was ashamed of my about-face, which could have stemmed, I thought, only from physical cowardice — the beatings. I was ashamed of my inexplicably rude behavior, ashamed of the pain and trouble I had caused my father. Ashamed and regretful that I might have saved us two years of suffering had I stuck to my original desire. *I was only a child,* I would think, *only twelve,* but then think, *Yes, but children make moral decisions. Children can be brave or cowardly.* And I'd know I'd been cowardly.

When I read the file after his death, alone in a room, I find the missing piece. Simple.

In his handwriting is a brief note on yellow paper, and then a typed letter to the lawyer, detailing something I told him before I ceased speaking, something I cannot recall — two threats I cannot remember ever knowing, even now that I have read and reread them many times.

Our stepfather told us that, because of the way the law worked, if the custody case was not resolved immediately, Tony and I would be separated and put into foster homes. And the case wouldn't be resolved directly, he said, because our mother was stupid enough to want us, and he himself would fight it, for the sake of Jehovah's name and for the sake of our spiritual well-being. Tony and I might never see each other again, depending on how things worked out. Secondly, if our father were ever so much as one minute late to drop us off from any visitation, he would be imprisoned for kidnapping. Our stepfather would call the police himself. He told us these things. Our mother, who knew better, had not disputed them.

Within days (as the file documents), my behavior changed utterly. I whistled when my father spoke. I sneaked apples into the bathroom and ate them there alone, so as to not eat a meal with him. He found the gnawed cores in the trash.

I must have believed that my obedience was protecting my brother and my father. But this belief, that childish anguish, is buried beyond my memory's reach.

How easy I was to read, to manipulate; how easy it must have been for my stepfather to see what I loved most and would surrender for.

After I ran away to live with my father, we never talked of this, because we never talked of any of it. It took two decades and his death to learn it, to understand the mysterious change of heart of the child I used to be.

I grew into a quiet woman. Restrained, reserved. Unreadable, says an acquaintance. A poker face, my closest colleague calls me. Watchful.

A woman, perhaps, without much personality.

21

After my brother and I had left and our stepfather was convicted and sent to the penitentiary, our mother was free. According to religious doctrine, his sexual misconduct had released her from their marriage.

Later, in college, I heard that our stepfather had been released from prison early, for good behavior. Disfellowshipped because of the criminal conviction, he was reinstated into the religion; a sincere apology to the elders was all that was required. After that, we heard nothing except that he had moved out of state and remarried.

Our mother went to nursing school. She's a nurse and hospital administrator somewhere — and is married again, to a Jehovah's Witness, a former elder, a gentle-voiced man who doesn't mind her job. They go out in service together.

We don't talk, though we have tried. I called her when my father died. Her card of sympathy was kind.

The songs from the softcover pink songbook come back to me sometimes, the melodies intact, the lyrics fragmented, missing words. Sometimes they play in my brain when I'm doing something, and it takes a while to realize what they are.

It used to frustrate me, but now I just sing them out loud, filling in the forgotten words with nonsense syllables, and they go away.

During the year after my father's death, I lived a kind of double life. In the daytimes, I taught my classes, wrote articles, served on committees, talked with Grey about his homework, did laundry and ironing. I earned tenure, won a research grant, took a class of students to England to study Woolf, Forster, and Lawrence. We saw Rooksnest, the real-life Howards End where Forster rode his pony as a boy, and walked down to the River Ouse.

But at home, I sat on the floor of the shower, sobbing in the dark heat. In bed, I cried onto my husband's chest. When I could sleep, I dreamt about my father, arguing with him, making desperate deals, begging. He was still alive, his death had not yet happened, had never happened, and all I had to do, say, was the right thing, and I could save him, if I could figure out what it was. If I could be pretty enough. If I could say the smart thing.

All night I would struggle, and each morning I would wake up to discover him dead.

But it has been longer now. I am thirty-five. I have written this. The dreams have stopped. There is a sense of peace, of resolution. I can think about him without weeping. I think about all of it, now, without pain.

No matter how beautiful the houses of Marrakech or San Cristóbal may be, the safety and seclusion of walled gardens where things can grow in peace, there comes a time when you want to walk outside. One blue square of sky can come to seem too small a ceiling.

My mother was ruled by the fear of shame: shame in the fancy department stores, shame in front of the congregation. My father's shame at his failed marriage built a façade so thick he couldn't even let his children in, until it was too late. My parents tried to hide so many things.

Before I built a wall I'd ask to know/What I was walling in or walling out, says the speaker in Robert Frost's poem "Mending Wall," rebuilding the stone property line with his neighbor while questioning the needfulness of it all.

I have always known precisely what my barriers kept at bay. But now I wonder what I may have walled in.

I see that my silence has kept me safe, but it has kept me lonely. Sometimes you want to leave the jeweled perfection of your privacy, to walk out into the world, among people, with your history on your sleeve. Come what may.

It's all right that there are things you do not get over, not really. You just go on, knowing that the things you love could be stripped from you at any moment, remembering to love them now.

It makes you human. You try to be decent and treat people gently, knowing that they, too, have their scars and madnesses that, like yours, do not show.

GRATITUDE

To Colin Harrison and my husband, who helped urge this reluctant memoir into existence.

To generous first readers R. Douglas MacDougall, Edie Simms, and Steve Charles.

To my agent Mitchell Waters, for your belief, encouragement, and pitch-perfect ear.

To my editor Casey Ebro — young, smart, and fearless — for taking this chance, and to Roland Ottewell and Georgia Liebman, for making it a better book.

To fellow writers Erica Wiest, Lisa Linsalata, Deborah J. Hunter, and Jane Curry, for making my weeks drafting this at Norcroft so fruitful, and to managing director Kay Grindland and founder Joan Drury, for making Norcroft possible for so many women for so long.

To Nancy Leonard, who taught the Thinking through Narrative workshop at Bard College, and to my fellow writers there, including Margaret Gray, Bob Bires, Sue Biondo-Hench, Tom Carrigan, Lucy Seward, Maureen Lampidis, and especially Jennifer Campbell.

To Amy Benson, Samantha Chang, Ted Conover, and Danzy Senna for their guidance and encouragement at Bread Loaf; to

Maribel Sosa and David Schuman for the inspiration of their work; to Michael Collier and Devon Jersild, for making my visits possible; and to Laura Chappell-Brown and Bryn Chancellor, my hilarious and talented roommates.

To exceptional editors along the way: Richard Foerster, Farhat Iftekharuddin, Susan Ito, Tina Cervin, Craig Arnold, M. L. Williams, Grant Tracey, Robert McLaughlin, and Michelle Tea. You went above and beyond.

To Peter Madden and George Rabasa, for your encouragement and support.

To Nancy and David Orr, kind and illuminating hosts, and Rick Warner, Dan Rogers, Phil Mikesell, and Melissa Butler, for my central metaphor.

To Naomi Shihab Nye, Sharon Olds, Alice Walker, A. S. Byatt, Angela Carter, Dar Williams, Natalie Merchant, Jean Rhys, Katherine Mansfield, and Margery Latimer, for work that moves and sustains me.

To my teachers Ewing Campbell, Janet McCann, Larry Oliver, Paula Cooey, Norman Sherry, Mackenzie Brown, Carol Amos, and especially Pamela R. Matthews and Laura White, for all the little revolutions of mind.

To my many lovely colleagues and students here at Wabash, but especially Warren Rosenberg, mentor and friend, and student David Olan, 1980–2005, who was a joy to know.

To Sharon and Sonia, for the incredible warmth and courage of your permission.

To my father, for the puzzle you left me with and for the love and will to solve it: *I know you by heart. You are inside my heart.*

To my mother, who did the best she could, and to the many kind and lovely Jehovah's Witnesses I knew as a child.

To my wonderful aunts, especially Barb, for your support.

To Cara and Reza, for your enduring friendship.

To Jennifer, for all your help.

To the Herring, Robinson, MacDougall, Boldt, Brandt, Lane, Carlson, and Kuckkan families, for welcoming my brother and me as your own. We're not always easy people.

To my beautiful mother-in-law Ingrid, because I promised.

To my husband and my son, for love that passes understanding. Everything I look upon is blessed.

To my lovely and amazing brother Tony — who read and approved every last word — for everything.

To Cool Julie, for marrying him.

To Indigo Feliciano Castro, born April 2005, for love, hope, and the future.

And to Beth Loughney, mouthy girl, wherever you are.